Over the years I have learned tha. and all the things that have shaped us, and weaves them into a beautiful tapestry. He then takes this precious intertwining of life and puts it on display for the world to see. It's a testimony of His grace and love for us, and of His promise to work all things together for good (Romans 8:28). I also believe that God loves to shine through us individually, corporately, and in small and large ways, bringing us together for various reasons and different seasons to accomplish His will.

In their book, *Tapestry of Grace*, the different writers have joined their stories in order to share some of their most life changing experiences. I believe God is using these accounts as a way to show you that there is nothing you have or ever will experience that is beyond the love and healing power of Jesus. The focus of each story is Jesus and His willingness to meet the writer in her moment of need. In each narrative, the writer focuses on the goodness of God and His unfailing love. As you read through the pages, you will discover a Savior who takes every loss, grief, unmet expectation, and difficult situation and turns it into an opportunity for greater intimacy with Himself and the Father. He then uses them as stepping stones, creating a pathway for greater faith and a deeper witness.

None of the writers claim to have achieved perfection. Some of their scars are still noticeable but are seen through the lens of hope, love, and joy, lightened and softened by the hand of Jesus. Each one expresses her ever growing confidence in a God who sees, hears, and responds to our faintest cry, a God who will come even when we are too weak to cry out.

As you read, I trust that Jesus will begin to speak to your heart. I pray that He hears your cries, enters into your situations, and brings His life to bear on each. I hope that this book will be a catalyst to a clearer understanding of how much you are loved and cared about by God. Not only that, but I trust He will allow you to experience His love first hand in such a way that you never have to wonder whether or not He really loves you. If you are reading this book and do not know Jesus, I pray that He will begin to tug at your heart and lead you to a place where you can see Him for who He really is and then begin the best relationship of your life.

—REVEREND KIM BURKHART, D.MIN

Tapestry of Grace

A Manifesto for Women
Scripture, Story & Self Application

Kristin Cash
& The Tapestry of Grace Writers
Watercolorist Jenn Hayes

Cover & interior design by Typewriter Creative Co.
Watercolor by Jennifer Hayes

Scripture quotations marked (NIV) are taken from the Holy Bible, New International Version®, NIV®. Copyright © 1973, 1978, 1984, 2011 by Biblica, Inc.™ Used by permission of Zondervan. All rights reserved worldwide. www.zondervan.comThe "NIV" and "New International Version" are trademarks registered in the United States Patent and Trademark Office by Biblica, Inc.™

Scripture quotations marked (CSB) have been taken from the Christian Standard Bible®, Copyright © 2017 by Holman Bible Publishers. Used by permission. Christian Standard Bible® and CSB® are federally registered trademarks of Holman Bible Publishers.

Scripture quotations marked (NLT) are taken from the Holy Bible, New Living Translation, copyright ©1996, 2004, 2015 by Tyndale House Foundation. Used by permission of Tyndale House Publishers, Carol Stream, Illinois 60188. All rights reserved.

Scripture quotations marked (NKJV) are from the New King James Version®. Copyright © 1982 by Thomas Nelson. Used by permission. All rights reserved.

Scripture quotations marked (ESV) are from The ESV® Bible (The Holy Bible, English Standard Version®), copyright © 2001 by Crossway, a publishing ministry of Good News Publishers. Used by permission. All rights reserved.

Scripture quotations marked (TLV) are from the Holy Scriptures, Tree of Life Version*. Copyright © 2014,2016 by the Tree of Life Bible Society. Used by permission of the Tree of Life Bible Society.

Scripture quotations marked (AMP) are taken from the Amplified Bible, Copyright © 2015 by The Lockman Foundation. Used by permission.

Scripture quotations marked (CEV) are from the Contemporary English Version Copyright © 1991, 1992, 1995 by American Bible Society. Used by Permission.

ISBN 978-1-7367388-0-1 (Paperback)
ISBN 978-1-7367388-1-8 (eBook)

A word of thanks...

First, this piece of my heart is dedicated to the Lord. May we truly honor Him by pointing the stories of our lives back to His faithfulness.

My husband Jimi, eternally supportive through the planning of this masterpiece.

My five, soon to be six, hooligans. You have been ever patient with your much distracted mama during this adventure.

My beautiful, talented team of writers at Tapestry of Grace Writers Guild. Kim, Mariel, Jana, Jennifer, Miriam, Barb, and especially Anita. This would have continued to live safely nestled away in the deepest pockets of my heart without your commitment and talent. I sincerely appreciate each of you.

Table of Contents

Foreword

You're opening a collection of sometimes messy but always honest accounts of redemption and grace, written by eight women who are all in the process of transformation because, whether we like it or not, God is in the transformation business.

We give him our old, He gives us His new like a caterpillar who starts out life slow and ugly and many-legged but God knows that's not all there is to the story. He imbues each caterpillar with the capacity for change, the ability to become a butterfly. But for change to manifest the caterpillar has to come away for a while, wrap herself in a cocoon, be still and let the transformation happen deep inside where no one can see.

In the fullness of time, she breaks free of the cocoon and she's been transformed into a completely different entity. God changes her into something altogether *else,* a new creature. She's unrecognizable from the caterpillar who was. The ugly legs are gone and she's sprouted colorful, glorious wings. She can cover so much more ground with those wings than she ever could with her many legs and feet. It's incredible and only God has the power to do this.

It's taken me a long time, years actually, but I'm *not* who I was and I know beyond a shadow of a doubt I'm a new creature in Christ. The desire to sin is waning. Oh, the *capacity* is still there and temptation rears its ugly head but as time goes on the desire to follow through weakens. I'm not perfect by any means, *(just ask my husband),* but my reaction when I'm hurt or betrayed or criticized is not what it was. I still *think* about it but I don't act on it like the old days.

When we get saved we receive Jesus' nature deep inside, a holy exchange takes place and we get *His* faith, *His* righteousness, *His* love, replacing our carnal nature. Over time we realize just how deeply we need Him *and how hopeless we are without Him.* There is *much* trial and error but keep in mind it's a walk, not a sprint.

He sanctifies and purifies and though we have all we need at the moment of true conversion, it takes time to comprehend just exactly what we have, all of its glorious height and depth and width and how to live and move and breath in it.

Yes, we all start out broken, sluggish, and messy, but…

…it's not where He leaves us.

Jesus takes our broken mess and in the flash of a nano-second says,

"I know all about your mess and I came for you anyway."

We can stay a big broken mess as long as we want, free will and all that, but He doesn't call us to stay there. He didn't *die* for us to celebrate our mess. *He died to give us the opportunity to become like Him.*

And He's not a mess.

We can let Him put all those broken pieces back together to become something new and beautiful. Our own messy masterpiece. He doesn't ask us to forget what broke us or caused our sticky mess. No.

He just takes away its power to define us.

He knows our history. But He won't let it define our destiny.

I only know one way to become more like Jesus and less like my mess and that's by spending time in His presence. I need to *know* Him. And I only know Him by taking the time to be still, each and every day. And stillness is hard, harder today than ever, it's hard to squelch the voices clamoring for our attention, hard to be okay doing nothing more than sitting in His presence leaving my laundry list of needs and problems, wants and issues behind. *Just being still.* Because stillness brings change. It's how we come to know him:

"Be still and know that I am God." Psalm 46:10

Eventually, we can look back on our former mess and embrace it for all it taught us. We will come to be grateful for it as we let Him cleanse us of its power.

We'll learn to forgive.

We'll learn to kiss the stones that bloodied our feet and love those who do not deserve our love. Because *He* did.

And we'll learn to forgive God for, we mistakenly thought, *not being there and letting us get broken in the first place.*

Years pass and our mess loses the power to define us. We find we don't need to stay there because the point of following Him is to become more like Him.

And He's not a mess.

Year by year we are transformed into His image. We become what we think about, because, "As a man thinks in his heart, so is he." Proverbs 23:7. And we start seeing the family resemblance. We can give power to our mess or strip it of everything that defines us, it's our choice.

It's time to stop being a broken mess because Jesus didn't die to make us "pretty messes". He makes us new creatures. Friend, you are NOT who you were!

Our messes and broken places are merely an illustration of His transforming power and redeeming love. Your life, your past, your sin, your transformation—all become an epistle written and read by men and your messy past becomes His masterpiece of grace.

You *were* a mess. You *now* are redeemed.
You *were* broken. You *now* are a new creation.
You *were* a sinner. You *now* are forgiven.

Which doesn't mean you won't struggle or have bad days or be tempted or sin ever again. You will. I do. *But.*

We can walk in newness of life, leaving our mess behind.

We can live how *He* lived.

And He's not a mess.

Let the words of these eight women stir you, touch you, and meet you exactly where you are. They are just like you and me. Their stories are real and God has met them in their broken places and brought healing and redemption, grace and peace in their hard seasons of pain and loss. They've found a way through and God is transforming them.

Through their stories of hope, as you allow Him access to your heart and submit to His deep lessons, you *will* gain intimacy with Him. As He takes you through and you find He *comes through,* you will gain firsthand knowledge of His faithfulness, you'll hear His heartbeat and He will send you out to bring comfort, healing and hope to other bleeding, messy souls.

—Kate Battistelli, author of *The God Dare*

Getting to know your authors...

KRISTIN CASH

Kristin is a mama to five, soon to be six, hooligans, and two angel babies. She is a sourdough enthusiast, lover of words, and a certified labor doula who is wildly passionate about helping women regain their sense of self worth and confidence. Kristin has written devotionals, a traditional blog, and community outreach articles focusing on self worth, overcoming an eating disorder, surviving pregnancy loss, homeschooling, and living your most authentic life now. She is the Founder of Tapestry of Grace Writers Guild and has the sincere honor and privilege of working with some of the sweetest and most talented women authors you will ever find.

Stay connected with Kristin at www.krisccash.com.

KIM BEAUMONT

After packing up their lives into one suitcase each, Kim and her husband Steve, with their youngest son Cody, moved from Australia to Redding, California in 2012. Knowing in their hearts that their family's legacy was about to change forever, as they ran after the call of God on their lives. They left behind two children in college, three dogs, two cats, and a retired horse.

An ordained pastor for 15 years, as well as a business owner with her husband for 25, Kim is passionate about seeing people activated and released into who God originally created them to be, resulting in lives filled with freedom, purpose, and joy.

Today Kim's life is full teaching and training upcoming leaders and developing a variety of future resources. She and Steve live on a little piece of heaven with their 3 dogs, 5 chickens and Nigel the cat. While learning to live authentically with the tension of pain and joy after the tragic loss of their youngest son.

Through story, whether written or spoken, Kim lives with eternity forever on her mind, whilst being real and raw in the midst of it all.

Stay connected with Kim at www.kimbeaumont.co.

MARIEL DAVENPORT

The Lord first captured Mariel Davenport's heart through His written Word. As a former atheist saved by reading the Bible, she has spent over twenty years studying and teaching God's Word. She inspires women to know the Word for themselves and tend their life by it, as tending a garden, little by little. Jesus ministers to her heart as she meditates on Truth while tending her backyard garden on the coast of North Carolina. Here He teaches her how He is tending her-pruning, nourishing, watering and by His grace, harvesting good fruit. Through the joys and trials in her own roller coaster marriage to her beloved, Mike, and homeschooling their two nearly launched boys, along with the staggering grief of losing her Dad, the Lord has taught her how to press into His Word in simple, applicable ways. As one easily given to fear, insecurity and worst-case scenarios, God is teaching Mariel through His Word, how to anchor her heart in Him. And she invites you to journey with her to grow in the grace and knowledge of our Lord and Savior Jesus Christ (2 Peter 3:18). Having written for online and print magazines like Proverbs 31, Living by Design and CBN.com, along with a new e-book study (30 Day to Communing with God: Reading, Unpacking and Practicing Biblical Prayers), Mariel has reached ladies of all ages and denominations with the joy of knowing God through His Word. She can be found online at marieldavenport.com, where she candidly shares the joys and struggles of applying the Word to every aspect of life and offers free tools for others seeking to dig into God's Word at marieldavenport.com/bonus. She is active on several social media platforms like Instagram at @marieldavenport and Facebook @marieldavenportauthor.

JANA FRALEY

 Jana Fraley is a Wyoming ranch wife, mom, and Christian writer. When not writing you will find her hunting and camping with her family, riding and working cattle with her husband, having deep faith conversations over coffee with her adult daughter, helping her son with 4-H projects, or cheering him on in the rodeo arena. She has a heart and passion for encouraging women in seeking an authentic and active faith in Christ. She loves journeying together with women of all ages as they discern Biblical truth, learn to apply God's Word with a Biblical Worldview and dive deeper in knowing what they believe.

You can find her writing at:

rusticandredeemed.com
www.facebook.com/janamaccarrie
www.instagram.com/rusticandredeemed

JENNIFER HAYES

Jennifer Hayes is Mama to three re= lentless honey badgers, beautiful, hilarious, children, a blogger/writer, artist and High School English Teacher. She is passionate about helping women cultivate a heart and home of peace by finding their true identity in Jesus and discovering beauty in the life they didn't expect. Jennifer has a Bachelor's Degree in Education with a Major in English and a Minor in subduing hostile-sibling-shenanigans. She also has an honorary PhD in baking. When she isn't writing or painting, you can find her in her favourite place- curled up with a hot coffee, her Bible, and Jesus...or hiding in the closet eating chocolate.

You can find her work at:

wellwords.ca
www.instagram.com/jennibell1980/
www.jennmakesitwrite.com

MIRIAM KOOK

Miriam Kook is a writer of both words and music. She collaborated as composer and music director with playwright and lyricist Steffi Rubin on a play about adoption called "My Other Mother" which enjoyed two staged readings in the Maryland area. She music directed a staged reading and collaborated as composer with writer and lyricist Ben Kintisch on his new hospice musical called "Life Review." She is currently writing the book, music, and lyrics to her own musical about the early loss of her father called, "The Broken Chord." She has written a memoir called, "The Long Way Home: Father Lost Father Found" and has contributed to a book being published this year called, "Sweet Tea for the Soul: Comforting Real Life Stories for Grieving Hearts." She is a member of Hope*Writers and TheaterMakers. She has music directed, accompanied and acted in community theaters and for high schools in New York City, Maryland, Israel, and Egypt. Credits include "West Side Story," "Bye Bye Birdie," "Chicago," "Guys and Dolls," "Hairspray," "Lion King," "Godspell," and "Beauty and the Beast." She volunteers for a local hospice where she plays and sings piano for residents and she also collaborates with children who have cancer to write songs about topics they enjoy. She and her husband Doug are Jewish believers in Jesus and they have a wonderful story to tell, which you can find on YouTube ("The Kooks Met Messiah"). She has three children and six grandchildren who give her so much joy. She gives thanks to God for opening her eyes to see His love for her and for giving her Doug, her wonderful family, and the lovely ladies who contributed to this devotional.

You can find some of her works at:

www.miriamkook.com
www.lifereviewmusical.com
soundcloud.com/miriam-kapell-kook

BARB LOEWEN

Barb Loewen grew up in a Christian home on the prairies of Saskatchewan, Canada. In 2003, she followed God's call to serve in missions at an MK school in Germany for two years. Her first year back home was a challenging one but she learned to trust God in a whole new way. He took her back into ministry working at a small Bible college in southern Saskatchewan. When the college started a second campus in British Columbia, Barb moved west to work at the Bible camp which was hosting the college. After helping with the first graduation three years later, Barb once again followed as God led her back to the mission organization with whom she had served before. This time she was ministering at home in mobilization, helping others get to the field. For 12 years, Barb had been mentoring college students as she had served at the college, the camp and her first three years with the mission. God gave her a vision for mentoring within the mission, caring for those members on the field. She transferred to member care to oversee the development of a mentoring program. She loves discipling women who are ministering overseas. She feels privileged to be able to walk alongside these faithful servants who have said yes to God, encouraging them and pouring into their lives as they pour into others. She has also taken on a role in the finance department with the mission in order to serve the Canadian members in that capacity. She loves living in the Shuswap and feels blessed to have an amazing view of mountains and a lake just outside her window—the fulfillment of a long-held dream. She began a blog when she rejoined the mission organization, and she writes on it as she has time.

Find her writing at www.obedienceandcliffjumping.wordpress.com.

ANITA STAFFORD

Anita Stafford loves to share with people that she is a daughter of The King, a wife, mother, grandmother, farmer, health coach, personal trainer, runner, powerlifter, and writer. One of her spiritual giftings is that of a scribe. It is a privilege to her to hear words from God and write them down to help educate, bless, and edify others. In 2015, after taking an honest look at the state of her body, health, and fitness, she began a personal health journey that has taken her from couch-potato to running a marathon in 2019, ten half marathons, a 10K and a power-lifting competition to date. During the journey, she found a passion to help other people turn their health and wellness around and went to school to become a health coach and personal trainer. Anita believes that we all have God-given assignments in life and she wants to help each person achieve their optimal holistic health (mind, body, and soul), so that they can fulfill those assignments. While her primary focus is health and nutrition, she believes that you cannot ignore the other parts of our life that nourish us as well, such as faith, career, and relationships. The idea for her approach to health coaching was born based on the scripture found in 3 John 1:2 that says "Beloved, I pray that you may prosper in all things and be in health, just as your soul prospers" NKJV. The name of her business, *Thrive Wellness with Anita*, came from the quote by Maya Angelou that says, "My mission in life is not merely to survive, but to thrive—and to do so with some passion, some compassion, some humor and some style." Anita has also always loved the written word, filling up countless journals with devotions, sermon notes and the words of God. Besides the contributions to this devotional book, she is working on several other written projects, including a series of children's books. Her prayer is that as you journey through this devotional with us, God speaks to you in a real and tangible way. As you read, may you find yourself even closer to Him and be strengthened in your heart, mind, body. and soul.

Preface

Hello, reader! I am thrilled you stumbled upon this piece of my heart. I have been dreaming of this moment for as long as I can remember. I would love nothing more than to sit down to a hot cup of coffee with you and share our stories; stories of God's faithfulness around every bend; stories that point back to the goodness of God. But, meeting like this will just have to suffice. It is a gift, nonetheless.

"And they overcame him by the blood of the Lamb, and by the word of their testimony" Revelation 12:11.

When I am walking through a valley, the last thing I consider is how my situation is going to impact the lives of those around me. Usually, my knees can be found firmly planted on the floor, tear stained cheeks, and the whisper of persistent, hopeful prayers filling the room. It isn't until I'm visited by hindsight that I begin looking for opportunities to share my story, my testimony, about how God met me in my need, walked me through it, and remained victorious.

I cannot tell you how many times my stories have been met by a weary hearted soul who needed to know they weren't alone, that God still cares, and that miracles still happen. Sharing my testimony gave them courage to keep praying, keep fighting for the victory and keep trusting that God is good.

By God's grace, and through a series of unexpected events, I came across seven talented women in my Hope*Writers community who shared the same passion to see the transformative stories of their lives bring glory to God, and hope to another, and so our journey began.

Each piece of this devotional has been prayed over. It is my sincere hope that in the pages of this book, you find the hope, encouragement, or miracle you are praying for. A reminder that God still sees you, that He hasn't forgotten you, and that He is shaping your testimony for your best and His glory.

Grab your favorite mug and settle into that corner, sun-drenched chair. You hold in your hands ninety sacred testimonies of life, love, loss and lessons. It is an honor to share them with you. To God be the glory.

Love, Kristin

Breakfast with Abba

When I am afraid, I put my trust in You.

Psalm 56:3 (NIV)

My father served in the Army most of my childhood. A noble and selfless act I knew firsthand. It was a stressful career that brought on more anguish than most would care to admit. A soldier carries weights not their own. Fortitude and integrity are badges of honor for men and women in uniform, who spend more nights worrying about the call of duty than not.

My father served in Special Operations. It was unpredictable and turbulent. He wasn't able to share his deployment schedule, let alone call while on mission. I remember feeling helpless, timid, and small when considering what my morning might look like. When duty called, he would discreetly pack in the middle of the night and quietly slip out before the first rays of light. Often, I would wake up and run to the living room, hoping to find him eating Raisin Bran at the kitchen table. Often, his seat was empty. I never blamed him. I missed him. Terribly.

Timid. Reserved. Unsure. This type of lifestyle formed character traits in me that 30 plus years later, I am still uncovering and giving to Jesus. Your fears do not define you, they just confine you, until you recognize their presence, and take it to prayer.

I was five years old the first time I walked in my sleep. There were mornings my father would come out into the living room to hastily grab his meticulously organized duffles just before slipping out the door, only to find the contents thrown all over the living room. I did this. In my sleep. I disassembled the one thing I subconsciously knew might keep him home. But it never did.

For years, this was my reality. Falling asleep afraid, frantically sleepwalking at some point during the night, waking unrested and no less afraid. No father there to tell me it would all be okay. Fear seemed to follow me like a companion; an unwelcome shadow.

When I was ten years old, my father came to my room and told me he needed me to have something very dear to him, but if he were to give it to me, he needed my assurance it would be treated honorably, and I would allow it to work its way into my heart. Moments later, he handed me a well-worn Bible, gold embossed name on the bottom right corner. His personal study Bible. Taking it from him slowly, it felt heavier than the words it held. It felt like the weight of privilege mingled with courage and peace. It felt like a refuge from the storms.

He told me, through weary eyes, that God never leaves. He never has to walk away. He is steadfast, faithful, and true. God would be my Abba when my Daddy had to leave. He would be there for me when no one else could. He would never let me down, leave me afraid, meek and small. He would guide me, guard me, and hem me in.

From that moment on, I read my Bible every morning before the bus came. Although many poor choices and trials still followed that commitment to the Word. Although I wandered away, stumbling in the night, He was faithful, steadfast and true, waiting for me, every morning at the kitchen table, ready to fill me with love, again.

Author: Kristin Cash

REFLECTION QUESTIONS

In what ways has God carried you through a season of fear?

What verse(s) have been of encouragement to you during these seasons?

How have you wandered away from Abba and how has He remained faithful?

His Protection

I will say of the Lord, 'He is my refuge and
my fortress, my God, in whom I trust.'

Psaln 91:2 (NIV)

'Because he loves me,' says the Lord, 'I will rescue him;
I will protect him, for he acknowledges my name. He
will call upon me, and I will answer him; I will be with
him in trouble, I will deliver him and honor him.'

Psalm 91:14-15 (NIV)

had been visiting my brother and his family for the weekend and was now
headed home, a couple of hours drive away. It was beginning to get dark.
It was fall, harvest time on the prairies, and I was driving on a highway
that was not usually very busy, especially at night. Coming toward me was a
line of trucks with harvesting equipment on flatbed trailers. I was driving a
small car and something in me wanted to give them extra room, so I moved
over to my right. I met one truck after another. Then one more passed and as
it did, suddenly I heard a loud bang and my front left tire immediately went
flat. I slowed down and pulled off to the side of the road. When I got out, I
saw that something had cut through the front left fender of my car, sliced the
tire, and crinkled my driver's door. This was before everyone had cell phones
so calling for help was going to be difficult.

It wasn't long though before a half-ton truck, also coming from the other
direction, slowed down, turned around, and came up behind me. The driver
got out and immediately asked me if I was okay. He was part of the harvesting crew. He said that the truck driver had seen my car go by, had heard the

bang, and was afraid he had killed someone!! He had immediately grabbed his radio and asked if someone behind him could see what had happened. Soon a police car arrived along with the supervisor of the crew. That's when I found out more details of what had happened. The trailer had a metal rod that slid into a cylinder along the back of the trailer, part of a ramp that they used to load the equipment. As they traveled, the rod had gradually worked its way out of the cylinder. Because it was getting dark outside, no one could see that this was happening. As I met the trailer, the rod struck my car and the damage was done.

They got my spare tire on, we exchanged information, and I was on my way. As I continued on my trip home, I began to wonder. What would have happened had I not moved over to give that extra space between me and the trucks? That rod would have extended much further into my car than just shearing off the fender and crinkling my door. I wondered if I would have made it home that night at all. To this day I believe that it was God's protection that got me home safely.

Many of us have times in our lives when we are certain that God intervened to keep us from harm. I am certain that there are also many days when we are completely unaware of the dangers that come close but never actually reach us. And yet, for many people, this isn't their story. Their story is of the danger that did touch them and changed their lives forever.

We don't know the reasons why God chooses to spare some people and not others. It's easy to look at Psalm 91:14-15 and ask, "Why didn't you protect and deliver me, Lord, as You promised in these verses?" But look again at the promises listed. As I look at them, I wonder if these promises are intended for different situations. Perhaps one time He rescues us, another time He protects and delivers us. And perhaps those times when danger does touch us are when the promise "I will be with him in trouble" is the one that we can claim.

Psalm 91:2 says. "He is my refuge and my fortress, my God, in whom I trust." I am so thankful that I can rest in this truth. No matter what may happen to me – whether I am protected from danger or I face trouble knowing that God is right there with me – I am so thankful that I have a God I trust, a God in whom I can find refuge no matter what is happening in my life at the moment.

Author: Barb Loewen

REFLECTION QUESTIONS

When has God protected you from danger or delivered you from trouble?

What trials have you faced knowing that God was with you in the midst of them?

What does it mean for you to trust God as your refuge and fortress?

The Power of Perspective

And God raised us up and seated us with him
in heavenly places in Christ Jesus.

Ephesians 2:6 (NIV)

I love chickens. Or like we call them in Australia, chooks! At the moment, I have five. Penny, who was originally the other half of Henny, but she died in her sleep. Bossy Beryl, the top of the pecking order. Hence her name. And Marge, Myrtle and Dottie, named after three of my great aunts. They give me so much joy as they cluck and chatter around my feet as I hang out our laundry on the washing line. That's another thing I love! Washing lines. Yes I know you're probably thinking, who is this strange woman? Here in Northern California, hardly anybody has a washing line. I know, shocking right? We live in one of the top 10 sunniest places in the US, according to google. And yet people use their clothes dryers. So weird. When we bought our house here, the first thing I did was put up a washing line. I was so excited! It felt just like home.

Anyway chickens. I love chickens. I love raising them, I love the eggs and I love eating them. Not my ladies of course, but others for sure. One of the things I have noticed about chickens is how focused they are as they scratch and peck and go about their day. They have their heads down completely intent on what is right in front of them. So much so that they often don't notice what is going on around them. I lost Doreen that way, when a hawk swooped down... but that is another story.

Here's the thing, I think we can be a lot like chickens. We can get so focused on what is happening in our lives, especially on our problems and situations that are worrying us that we only see what is right in front of us.

As Christians we are called to a higher perspective. Not just to see from that higher perspective, but to live from there.

Ephesians 2:6 is not just a theological or doctrinal reality. It is a spiritual truth. We are spirit beings in a physical body. And as we learn to live by the spirit, and with the spirit in Christ Jesus we will see from a far greater perspective.

Rather than living like a chicken, only aware of what is right in front of us. We can live like eagles! They can see more than eight times the distance than that of a human being . Spotting a rabbit between two or three miles away. Their perspective is so much wider and greater than my chickens and of us for that matter.

As we partner with the Holy Spirit, We have the ability to see from his perspective. But too often we get caught up in the worries and concerns of the moment and it can overwhelm us. We unconsciously begin to partner with fear and anxiety, listening too much to our own self talk and the whispers of the enemy as he leans into our ear.

We have a choice. We can continue to act and see like a chicken. Or we can take a step back and look from God's perspective. And see from a much broader view, a bigger picture. And as we lean into Him, he shows us by the spirit what is happening. How much better could our lives be, if we learned to consistently live and see from God's perspective? Even in the mystery and uncertainty he always has a solution!

I don't know about you, but I would rather see things from his perspective, than my own. So as much as I love my chickens, I know which perspective I want.

What about you? Are you a chicken or an eagle?

Author: Kim Beaumont

REFLECTION QUESTIONS

What situation at the moment do you need God's perspective on?

When you look from the heavenly perspective what do you see?

My Way, the Highway, or God's Way

PART ONE

A man's heart plans his ways,
But the Lord directs his steps.

Proverbs 16:9 (NKJV)

I was about seven or eight years old when I began mapping out my life. I was a dreamer with a vivid imagination as a little girl, and would often share my life plans with my mother as she cooked dinner: I was going to marry Georgie, the boy from the neighboring ranch, we'd have six kids and all their names would start with the letter "K." We'd live in a single wide trailer house within a few feet of the old ranch house I grew up in, where our front door would face their backdoor, and we would all live happily ever after.

It was a beautiful plan; and although parts of it changed as I grew up, parts of it remained the same. I had to give up on the idea of marrying Georgie because he never saw me as anything more than his little sister's pesky friend, my dream house changed from a trailer house to a large ranch house, and my mother convinced me that living right next door wouldn't be as much fun as I thought it would be. Yet, my life-mapping tendencies were still the same as when I was a little girl, they were just more realistic. I eventually met and married my husband, Mike, we moved across the state from my parents, and although he shared the dream of having children, we settled on two or three kids instead of six.

During those early days of marriage, I would spend my morning Quiet Time sharing with God what my plans were. I wasn't praying as much as I was telling God how I thought my life should go: Someday we'd move back to one of our family's ranches and we'd spend our days raising cattle and kids. Married for two years, then baby number one, and two years later baby number two would join our family. Twins would be great because then I wouldn't have to convince Mike to have that third child. I was willing to leave that part up to God if He was willing to leave the rest of the planning up to me. Life was good and I was happy... as long as He did things my way.

At first everything was going according to plan; within a week of celebrating our second anniversary, Hannah MacCarrie was born and my journey as a mother began. Becoming a mother was everything I thought it would be as I realized this was the purpose God designed me for. I envisioned the little brothers or sisters that would join Hannah someday; and I was filled with joy thinking about the life Mike and I would create, raising cattle and kids. However, this was where my plans took a sudden detour and God began to shape and mold my faith in Him, and not in my dreams. Instead of another baby coming two years later, it would take 11 years before we had another child. Getting back to ranching took even longer. Living next door to my parents would never happen.

All my plans slowly began to unravel, and disappointment defined my life. Comparison was my worst enemy. I couldn't go to our local Moms Group without dissolving into tears as yet another friend announced her pregnancy. I questioned why God wasn't answering the prayers of my heart, but He was others. I would paste on a fake smile and choke back tears, becoming more miserable every day. I was eaten with jealousy towards friends who were raising their children on family ranches, I missed the lifestyle and I missed being close to my parents. I became angry at God because He wasn't answering my prayers the way I thought He should. You see, not only was I a dreamer with a great imagination, but I also had a control issue. I struggle with an "It's my way or the highway" sort of attitude. I had the need to feel in control, and I believed that God would bless the plans I made. But God... in His unending grace and mercy, God knew this tendency to control would be the cause of many heartaches, wounded relationships, and devastating disappointments. When I look back, I recognize this is where He began a refining work in my life, using the heat of those disappointed plans of mine and burning away the dross of my need for control. What has resulted is a faith that recognizes the grander perspective of God's sovereignty and plans in all areas of my life. He brought me to a crossroads where I had to choose His will or my way.

Author: Jana Fraley

REFLECTION QUESTIONS

Have you struggled with control, with an "It's my way or the highway" kind of attitude?

How has the need for control negatively affected you and those around you?

Can you recognize a refining process that God is using in your life to combat any tendencies to control situations or people in your life?

My Way, the Highway, or God's Way

PART TWO

For this child I prayed, and the Lord has granted
me my petition which I asked of Him.

1 Samuel 1:27 (NKJV)

For years I made plans that didn't work out, facing brick walls of discouraged dreams and unmet expectations. Dealing with disappointment was exhausting and discouraging. I was diagnosed with endometriosis and struggled through years of infertility, surgeries, hormone treatments, and miscarriage. Barrenness defined me, and I related to the women in the Bible that faced infertility: I lacked faith like Sarah, became bitter like Rachel, and sorrowed deeply like Hannah.

Then, in late January of 2007, I was finally pregnant again. Mike and I were ecstatic but cautiously optimistic because of previous disappointments and decided not to tell anyone except a couple close friends. A few days after finding out I was pregnant, I woke up early in the morning with excruciating pain, overcome with the fear of losing another baby. Any hope I had the day before was now crushed.

I ended up in the emergency room of our small-town hospital where they thought I was suffering from an ectopic pregnancy. I overheard the doctor say, "This is a non-viable pregnancy, we'll have to terminate". I couldn't process what that meant; physical pain and soul anguish washed over me. I immediately began grieving, and no longer had the energy for hope. I was in and out of consciousness and felt as if I were being tossed back and forth in an angry sea. As I heard disjointed voices around me discuss the probable outcome of the situation, I felt helpless in my inability to be part of the conversation. I couldn't think, I couldn't pray, I couldn't muster up more than that little mustard seed of faith; and even that felt lost and carried along by those violent waves of grief and pain.

Eventually my doctor came into the room and told us that he was sending me to another hospital; he just couldn't be certain this was an ectopic surgery because the ultrasound equipment in our little hospital was outdated and it was too early for a tubal pregnancy to cause this amount of pain. I was taken by ambulance to a larger hospital in the next county, and within an hour of being admitted I had a more advanced ultrasound. They discovered the pregnancy was still viable, and instead it was a cyst on my ovary that ruptured, causing incredible pain as I bled internally. We still weren't out of the woods; the ovary would possibly have to be removed and there was a high chance the baby wouldn't survive the surgery.

But with those words that little seed of faith implanted itself into my heart and hope began to grow. I gave the child and myself completely to God, knowing that He was not working against my plans, but was working out a plan of His own. I asked Mike to grab my Bible and pray over me and the baby; the physical pain was still too intense for me to pray for myself, so my sweet husband interceded on our behalf.

A couple days later as Mike wheeled me out of that OB department, he warned against getting my hopes up. But my hopes were already up, my faith and trust stronger. I told him, "We'll be back here in these halls in 9 months, to meet our precious baby, I just know it." And nine months later, Kade Micheal was born with a beautiful intensity that has filled our lives for going on 13 years now.

I can't help but look at my son and see proof of God's amazing design. Those years of unfulfilled hope and expectations didn't define me, they refined me, strengthening and purifying my faith and trust in God's plans and purposes. I had to ask myself amid all my disappointed plans and dreams, would God still be God, and would He still be good, even if He didn't answer my prayers my way? Would I still choose His way over my way, and praise Him in the midst of disappointments and pain; or would I choose to walk away from Him because He didn't answer the way I wanted Him to?

God carried me through those disappointments and pain and brought me to a place where my greatest desire is walking through this life with Him, no matter what happens to my plans. My relationship with Him has grown stronger and more mature, and my greatest plan is for my life to reflect Jesus. Plans that come to fruition aren't life's biggest blessings; the best gift He gives is the understanding that, no matter what happens in my life, He is working out His plans and purposes for my good and His glory.

Author: Jana Fraley

REFLECTION QUESTIONS

When is a time that you have faced unmet expectations or frustrated dreams?

Have you had to give up on a dream that wasn't in alignment with God's plan for your life?

How have you found God to be more able than you are to direct the paths of your life?

You Shall Go Out With Joy

PART ONE

Seek the LORD while he may be found;
call upon him while he is near;
let the wicked forsake his way,
and the unrighteous man his thoughts;
let him return to the LORD, that he
may have compassion on him,
and to our God, for he will abundantly pardon.
For my thoughts are not your thoughts,
neither are your ways my ways, declares the LORD.

Isaiah 55:6-9 (ESV)

A s parents we hope and pray that we can do a good job at parenting each child and that they can grow up to have happy and productive lives. My son Aaron was my easiest birth and the most outgoing of my children. As a little boy, he had a vivid imagination and could "watch" movies on a blank wall, a wall that was blank to me but to him, it was alive with the dancing of Riff and the Jets from the show, "West Side Story" with the music blaring out, "When you're a Jet, you're a Jet all the way from your first cigarette to your last dying day." He loved talking to strangers, putting on magic shows, singing into a microphone, making birthday cakes out of playdough, and playing with his pretend friend, Monster George.

One thing Aaron seemed to excel at was acting. His first role was Tar Baby in a play about "Brer Rabbit" which we put on when his Dad and I were working at a sleep away camp in the Catskill Mountains of NY. Aaron didn't have a big part but he was the hit of the show. He, as Tar Baby, needed to be covered with tar. So, we put him in a box and smooshed chocolate pudding all over him. He was only 3 years old but he sat perfectly still in the box covered in chocolate pudding and waited for his turn. On a specified cue, he jumped up in the box and displayed his chocolate pudding self. The audience full of kids roared with laughter, erupted in applause, and for five minutes straight clapped and yelled, "Aa-ron, Aa-ron, Aa-ron!" Aaron stayed in character with his arms wide out and a big grin on his face. He ate up the applause and then enjoyed eating up the chocolate pudding that was all over him as soon as the play was over.

He did have his terrible two kinds of moments, but for the most part, he was a sunny, happy little boy. That is, until he went to school. There, things began to go downhill for him. First the teachers complained that he was not paying attention, that he was losing things, and forgetting assignments. Then he was having trouble with the other children because he was not considered cool, or athletic, and maybe he was a little goofy. Some teachers tried to help; others called him lazy and lacking motivation. By the time Aaron got to 4th grade, he was a pretty sad little guy. And I, his mother, was having a hard time figuring out how to help him.

Meanwhile, we had moved to Israel for work when Aaron started middle school. He and his sister attended an American International School, which had smaller classes and children from all around the world. It was a wonderful environment for Aaron. He started making friends and he seemed much happier in school and in life. However, he still struggled in his classes and was eventually diagnosed with Attention Deficit Disorder. He was prescribed medicine to help him but the medicine was rough and he became very moody. Something I didn't know about me was that I worshiped at the shrine of education. It is not a bad thing to want your children to be smart, to go to a good college. But you know something is an idol if your life feels like it is falling apart if you don't have that thing. Aaron was struggling in school and I began to feel like I was falling apart.

I was angry with Aaron a lot of the time. I resorted to nagging, threatening, begging, and finally to running around behind him to make sure he had everything he needed for school. He started going directly to his room and shutting the door every day when he returned from school. I had a terrible pain in my heart that turned into pity for him. I despised the feeling but it taunted me that my son was a loser in life and would never find his way. I felt like it was time to pray and get serious with God. I was afraid I would irreparably damage this son of mine if I did not figure out a better way to be his mother. I knew God had answers and I knew I needed them.

Author: Miriam Kook

REFLECTION QUESTOINS

Have you ever felt at a loss for how to handle a situation?

Why might being at a loss actually be a good thing?

You Shall Go Out With Joy

PART TWO

For as the heavens are higher than the earth,
so are my ways higher than your ways
and my thoughts than your thoughts.
For as the rain and the snow come down from heaven
and do not return there but water the earth,
making it bring forth and sprout, giving seed
to the sower and bread to the eater,
so shall my word be that goes out from my mouth;
it shall not return to me empty,
but it shall accomplish that which I purpose,
and shall succeed in the thing for which I sent it.
For you shall go out in joy
and be led forth in peace;

Isaiah 55:10-12 (ESV)

Once in a while, when we come to the end of our rope, God will give us phenomenal help seemingly out of the blue. Aaron was about to start 7th grade and he wasn't very excited about school beginning again. The dread of all that renewed drama filled my heart with so much despair. I felt that I was doing a terrible job as a Mother and that my lack of a focused approach, and subsequent aimless method of coping with Aaron was shutting him down and causing him to withdraw from me and everyone else. Living overseas, I had many volunteer opportunities available to me that I

was excited about. But my heart was so heavy that I decided to put everything else aside to spend time with God on my bed, Bible open, praying for
wisdom and guidance for Aaron. Looking back, I am amazed that I had not
thought to do this before. But often, seeking God for the most important
issues in one's life is only seen as a last resort. No matter, I had finally come
to the conclusion that I was clueless about what to do for Aaron and that it
was time to get serious about asking God for help.

Following the advice of Philippians 4:6-7, I told God, through tears, about
Aaron and what had evolved in his life. I talked about his vibrant personality
that now seemed gone, like a bright sunny day that had disappeared behind
a black cloud. I talked about his shut door and his long-term school project
that he hadn't worked on or told me about until the day before it was due. I
talked about the mean person at school, the teacher who didn't like him, the
play he decided not to be in because he didn't get the lead part, and the close
friends who had moved away and had not been replaced. I thanked God for
His involvement in Aaron's life, His complete knowledge of Aaron as His
Creator, and His good plans for Aaron. The more I thanked God, the more
hopeful I became. Then the Philippians passage encouraged me to make my
requests known to God. I told God that I wanted Aaron to have a good life
and asked for God to make plans for him that would lead to that very thing.
And I asked for wisdom for me and my husband so that we could be a part
of bringing that about.

The following day, I was back sitting on my bed and I turned to Isaiah 55
and it burst open for me on the subject of Aaron. It told me that I should
forsake my ways and thoughts because God's ways and thoughts were higher
than mine. I was ready because I could see that I had no earthly idea what
I was doing with Aaron and yet I kept doing it every day and it kept being
wrong. I read about rain and snow coming down and doing some amazing
things, things I could never do. I needed an outsider, a person with much
more insight, much more oversight, whose thoughts and ways with Aaron
were right. I needed God. And then it told me that the rain and snow which
God sent down made a lot of things happen in the world: flourishing, growing, seed provided for a sower, bread provided for an eater, God's desire and
purpose being accomplished. Curiously absent was any person. It all seemed
to proceed from and return to God, doing His will in the interim. Aaron's
life was pretty much between him and God. When God sent forth His Word
into Aaron's heart, it would have the desired effect. And the effect would be
that Aaron would go out with joy and be led forth with peace...

Finally, God instructed me that my role in Aaron's life was now to encourage him. I had to learn how to be an encourager. I made lists of everything positive I could say to him and the more I said those things to him, the more he started coming out of his room to talk with me. I realized he was so thirsty for someone to say encouraging things to him. This special season of God's instruction on the subject of Aaron has helped me understand how faithful God is to send His rain and snow down into situations when we realize our ways and thoughts are not sufficient.

Author: Miriam Kook

REFLECTION QUESTIONS

When you have been in what feels like a hopeless situation, what Bible verses have helped you?

How has God entered a situation in your life to infuse it with His wisdom? What has been the outcome?

Leaning on the Word

Trust in the LORD with all your heart, and do not lean on your own understanding. In all your ways acknowledge him, and he will make straight your paths.

Proverbs 3:4-5 (ESV)

On my knees, I was crying to the Lord in the dark corner of the closet, questioning my marriage and why He would allow us to get to this place. I had walked with Him, so had my husband. But now we had chosen our own flesh and desires over His. Life had come with a vengeance and we were unprepared. Now it felt as if the last fifteen years of marriage were swirling down as if into a drain and I couldn't hold on to it any longer.

The truth of Proverbs 3 came to mind like a flicker of hope in the distance. How could I trust God with all my heart when now I found my heart shattered all over this floor? I cried out for help to Jesus. He alone had the power to change my husband. And to change me. I knew marriage mattered to Him. But what about mine?

What is it that I am leaning on? What am I putting my weight towards?

I had spent the better part of the last decade teaching women to walk by the truths of the Word, yet here I was, stumbling and grasping for something that felt just out of reach. I stretched my hand out for the hem of Jesus' garment, begging for hope.

The days and weeks that followed were filled with cold shoulders and an unfamiliar icy silence. Our marriage now void of flirty texts and bedtime kisses. I felt alone in a house filled with people. I tried to sort through my pain, but the bleeding wouldn't stop. I searched for ways to numb the pain, to breathe again. I searched anywhere but God. The fleshy search kept me from His Word, from turning to Him, the weight of the guilt of my poor choices was too heavy to lift. I spiraled into darker places as I leaned on my own understanding. The weight of my own thinking was frail and unable to hold me up.

It was in the deep darkness that I suddenly felt the pull I could no longer ignore. The tugging on my heart had grown and one day I could deny it no longer. I reached for His hand by reaching for His Word and felt peace envelope me. I had been running for too long and was exhausted of trying to numb my pain on my own. To my surprise, His word came as a balm to my weary soul, not the condemnation I had expected. His kindness drew me, and I bawled for new reasons now. Grace, love, and forgiveness rushed in, filling me anew.

I wish I could say that the day the Lord got ahold of me, everything changed in my marriage, but it did not. But I changed. The Lord did graciously convict and work in and through my man, as well, in His own time. And through months of healing, long talks, forgiveness, and much grace, our marriage found healing in His Presence.

Not every story turns out like ours, but God does *always* seek to redeem and heal those who will choose to trust in Him over their own limited understanding.

Author: Mariel Davenport

REFLECTION QUESTIONS

Have you found yourself in a season of trying to lean on your own understanding and found it to be lacking?

How did you turn back to the Lord? Spend time in His Word today and ask Him for His peace that surpasses all understanding.

Come Unclean

Daughter, your faith has healed you. Go in
peace and be freed from your suffering.

Mark 5:34 (NIV)

'’ve been familiar with this verse my whole life. I’ve heard it quoted and
taught over and over again. It’s a foundational concept for the gospel, isn’t
it? Coming to Jesus, as we are. Many of us have heard this, but I wonder
how many of us actually *believe* it.

I think often about the bleeding woman Jesus heals in the gospels.

For generations, the law had declared anything and anyone who had come
into contact with blood to be “unclean.” A menstruating woman, (and everything she touched), was deemed “unclean,” and was to be kept separate
for a period of time before she could be purified; made clean again. It’s not
that being unclean was a sin against God, it just meant that to come into
contact with blood was to come into contact with death, and one could not
come into the presence of God with death on their hands and survive.

We cannot bring death into the presence of God.

I think about how humiliating it must have been, how demoralizing, how
exhausting, how devastating, going from doctor to doctor, spending all she
had searching for a cure that wouldn’t be found. And I’m sure everyone
in town knew the embarrassing details of her very personal struggle. How
degrading it must have been, having such private information served up
for consumption around dinner tables all over the neighborhood. How
lonely her own dinner table empty because the Law required her to keep
her distance.

Imagine the courage of this precious woman. She had been bleeding, *unclean*, for years... *years!* Likely having been taught all her life that she cannot come into a public place, *let alone the presence of God,* in this state. If the Levitical priests dared come into God's presence unclean, they would die. But this desperate woman pushed her way through a crowd and threw her unclean body at the feet of Jesus, grasping the clothes of the spotless Lamb. Unclean, and yet touching the very presence of the living God!

One would have expected a lightning bolt to strike her where she stood. At the very least, a rebuke for daring to touch the Holy One. But instead, her gentle Savior looked for her, the woman who had reached out for him, and he healed her, and called her daughter. Not a bolt of lightning. Not a harsh rebuke. A term of endearment, close familiarity. A loving reception. A willing restoration:

"Daughter, your faith has healed you. Go in peace and be freed from your suffering" (Mark 5:34).

Her faith is what healed her. *She believed.*

She believed his kindness was for *her.*
She believed it was *safe.*
She believed she could come to *him,* because he had come *for her.*
She came as she was. She came bleeding.

And there were others. So many others!

The bleeding woman came unclean.
The Samaritan woman came unfulfilled.
The adulterous woman came unfaithful.
The prostitute came unworthy and unwanted.
The Canaanite woman came undeserving.

And he received them. Blood, bruises, burdens and brokenness, he received them and restored them all.

Reading the beautiful stories of these precious women redeems my reluctance to come into Jesus' presence when I am "un"-*something.* Their stories are the antidote for shame when I find sin in my heart and death on my hands.

When I scream at my children.
When I resent my husband.
When I withhold my affection.

When I justify my harsh words.
When I cling to *being* right instead of *doing* right.
When I grapple for control.

The moments we need His presence most are moments we feel least worthy to be in it. Just like this woman, I need to push past the fear and reach for his presence, no matter what state I'm in. It's safe to believe He will embrace me with kindness and compassion, because the hem of his garment is where the healing is.

Author: Jennifer Hayes

REFLECTIONS QUESTIONS

What makes you feel "unclean?" Are there any other "uns" you are carrying?

Are you carrying a secret shame that is preventing you from fully entering into Jesus' presence? What is it?

Close your eyes and imagine yourself reaching for Jesus' hem. How does it feel when he turns towards you and calls you "daughter?" What else does he say to you?

Three Hundred Dollars
& Two Reindeer

Adonai—He is the One who goes before you. He will not fail you or abandon you. Do not fear or be discouraged.

Deuteronomy 31:8 (TLV)

The first week of January 2000, just a few days after Y2K came and went uneventfully, I packed what would fit into the back of an extended cab Ford F150 pickup and set out cross-country. Not for a vacation, but to escape. I was running from the abuse of a husband who refused to get help for his drug, alcohol, and anger issues. I was headed from California to Arkansas with no plan except to take one day at a time and pray that I and my two daughters, ages 3 and 5, got there safely.

I reached a breaking point that day when my husband had me backed up against the kitchen cabinets screaming at me because I had confronted him about drug paraphernalia that I found in my car. When I grabbed the phone to call 911, he yanked it away, smashing it to pieces on the floor. After more terrifying moments of pushing and shoving, he yelled that he was leaving to play golf, which was another of his outlets to drink and blow off steam.

I knew that a round of golf would give me about 2 hours, time enough to pack and get us somewhere safe from the verbal, mental, and physical abuse. It is amazing how quickly you can grab clothes, toys, toiletries, and other necessities when you are desperate. I piled what I could into the bed of the truck and covered it with a tarp. Inside the back of the cab, I made a play area of sleeping bags, pillows, coloring books, crayons, and toys, including the stuffed reindeer the girls received for Christmas.

Our first night away, I called my mom from the home of a friend where we stayed. She immediately wired some money to my bank account. I now had a total of $300. This was all we would have to make the nearly 1900-mile trip from Sacramento, California to Ozone, Arkansas, where my mom and sister lived.

The first order of business on Day One was to get a spare tire, which I found at a salvage yard. My $300 began to shrink. Thank God that he had prompted me to pack all kinds of snacks because I did not know how we would make that money last for gas, meals, and somewhere to stay.

Day Two, we left California heading east. We stayed that second night in a hotel (more money gone). Day Three we arrived at the home of family in Arizona and stayed there two days to recover and replenish snacks and supplies. Day Five, we set out again, crossing through New Mexico, headed further east.

Remember those two reindeer I told you about? Did I mention they were singing reindeer? When you pressed their front paw, they would begin to sing "We wish you a Merry Christmas" and their mouth moved to the song. Somewhere along the road, the girls thought it would be a great idea to try to get them to sing in sync with each other. Repeatedly, they pressed those front paws trying to get the music and words in perfect unison. Over and over and over. The temptation was great, somewhere along the highway in New Mexico, to throw those reindeer out the window. But they were keeping the girls happy and that was worth more than my sanity. At least that is what I kept telling myself as the miles fell away under our tires and the singing continued.

There were so many moments when God intervened with provision. Our last night on the road, somewhere in a town in Texas, a motel owner allowed me to pay for our room with my out of state check as our cash was dwindling and we had one more day on the road. He did not know me from any other stranger that night, but that friendly innkeeper had pity and gave us a room with only my check and a promise that it was good. Like the widow and her sons pouring oil into vessels, every time I counted the money in my wallet, I had enough for one more meal and one more tank of gas. Finally, late in the night on Day Seven we arrived home in Arkansas, safe and sound.

I do not know how $300 lasted all that way. I do not know what ever happened to those reindeer. Looking back even now, my girls remember a grand adventure. I remember stress, worry, and endless, anxious prayers. Prayers that were honored again and again on that trip with $300, two reindeer, two children, and one praying mama.

Author: Anita Stafford

REFLECTION QUESTIONS

Have you ever had to make a difficult decision very quickly?

Can you remember a time when God supernaturally met a need that you had?

What happened and how did God provide?

How have you seen God's hand of protection in your life?

Redemption after Trauma

The thief comes only in order to steal and kill and destroy. I came that they may have and enjoy life, and have it in abundance (to the full, till it overflows.)

John 10:10 (AMP)

When I was a young child, I vividly remember being carefree. I recall running in and out of clothes racks in department stores. And as I grew older, I remember being a joy seeker; looking for the happiest person in the room, and clinging to them like my life depended on it.

I wanted friends with freckles, who knew how to belly laugh, and eat room temperature string cheese in the middle of the night. Laughter felt safe and unpretentious. I felt rested and natural when I surrounded myself with friends who knew how to laugh. I found every legitimate excuse to be around a friend who could celebrate the mundane, and turn every dull moment into memory.

Laughter is a weapon against the enemy. It centers us and roots our souls in gratitude. And where gratitude makes residence, hope flourishes. The devil wants to rid our lives of any reason we might have to laugh.

Laughter faded from my eyes at a young age. Trauma does that to a woman. Regardless of age, being the victim of sexual assault will dissolve the laughter from a soul. Every moment after trauma becomes work.

I was 14 years old when "no" was ignored. I was barely having a regular monthly cycle when my reason for living became to protect my sister from two teenage boys who rode my bus, and regularly stole my dignity while threatening to destroy my reputation. Thirty plus years later and I am still bringing those memories to Jesus.

But daily, as I wake up with the weight of the world on my shoulders, I am reminded that God came, human as He was, that we might have and enjoy life. And not just survival, but abundance. Anything less would be tragic. Anything short of living a life of abundance is not what God had in mind for us as believers, daughters of the King.

When I face the reality of my trauma, and I consider who I am in Christ and who He says I am, I have the choice to lay it all before Him, because He goes before me, or I can continue carrying it, allowing the memories to mare my peace and my ability to laugh freely, and walk with my soul and my head held high.

Trauma doesn't instantly go away; and many women will tell you they never fully healed from sexual abuse. No amount of counseling can erase the memories made when someone shatters your dignity. But our memories do not define us, they refine us. Our memories can be the catalyst for deeper connection with Christ and become a witness to those who are desperately needing to hear they are loved, worthy, pure, spotless, redeemed, priceless, and chosen.

I am here, offering my memories to you as a token of courage. You can survive after trauma, because Christ came to give you life, and life to the fullest. My story, although discreetly offered, is a testimony of the goodness of God to see us through our valleys, and carry us to the higher places when we have fallen victim to the hands of another.

You may feel broken, but your wounds are covered by the Blood of the Lamb. I encourage you to reach out, share your story in safe and trusted places, and allow God to come into the places of your shame, guilt, and self- hatred so you can become free and live the life God has in store for you.

Author: Kristin Cash

REFLECTION QUESTIONS

If you have experienced trauma, have you invited God into the wounded places?

Have you reached out to safe and trusted sources for healing and hope?

If you know a friend who has endured trauma, how can you offer support?

I'm Not Enough

Therefore, I will boast all the more gladly about
my weaknesses, so that Christ's power may rest on
me. ...For when I am weak, then I am strong.

2 Corinthians 12:9-10 (NIV)

I was working at a Bible Camp where we also hosted a Bible College through
the school year. It was the end of summer and I was exhausted. God knew
what I needed so He arranged a few days rest for me at a local Bed &
Breakfast run by someone in my church. I didn't know her well at the time,
but she became part of God's blessing in those restful days and in the years
since. God used our conversations in my time there to show me a lie that I
was believing, and the truth that was a crucial part of it.

We were talking about core lies. Janine was telling me about a program that
God had used to help her see the core lie that she believed and how it had
affected much of her life. As we talked, God revealed to me that the core lie I
believed was "I'm not enough." It encompassed much of my life as I believed
I wasn't beautiful enough, thin enough, smart enough. You get the picture.
Perhaps you can even relate to those thoughts. As is so often the case when
God reveals things that have affected me for so long, the revelation took
time to process and take root. And God wasn't done with what He wanted to
show me about this lie that I believed.

As I turned this thought over and over in my mind, God showed me how
this thought, "I'm not enough" was a lie. God is the One who created me
– knit me together is how Scripture describes it – and as His creation I am
fearfully and wonderfully made (Psalm 139:13-14). Because of His sovereignty I can know that He made me as I am for a purpose. That means that I
am enough. I can rest in the knowledge that I am made as I am because this

is who God wanted me to be. That doesn't mean I shouldn't change or grow. I am a work in progress, certainly, but God made me as He did for a reason.

And yet, there is truth to this lie as well. The truth is that I am not enough, and I will never be enough because no one is enough. Romans 3:23 tells us "for all have sinned and fall short of the glory of God." That is why we need God's salvation. It is Jesus in us who makes us enough before God. It is His work on the cross, His shed blood that redeems us. It is His Spirit in us that continues to transform us. I am enough only because of Him. And so, I can rest in the truth that I am not enough on my own, but I am enough through Him.

As God showed me how this lie of "I'm not enough" was both a lie and the truth, He took me to Paul's recounting of his thorn in the flesh in 2 Corinthians 12. Paul teaches that it is in our weakness that we are made strong. If I thought that I was enough in and of myself, I wouldn't need to lean on God. I would be handling everything on my own and might even be doing a decent job of it. But my belief that I'm not enough pushes me to rely on the Lord. Paul even goes on to say that he delights in his weaknesses and difficulties. "For when I am weak, then I am strong" (2 Corinthians 12:10b). Paul tells us about the contrasts, the conflicting truths that exist in God's reality. Through Christ, it is in our weakness that we are strong.

God showed me my conflicting truths in the days following that revelation several years ago. The truth is that I am enough because I am who God created me to be. However, it is also true that I am not enough and will never be enough on my own. Christ makes me enough through His sacrifice and His power at work in and through me. I can rest in these conflicting truths and know that in all ways I am enough because of Jesus.

Author: Barb Loewen

REFLECTION QUESTIONS

What do you think might be a core lie that you believe about yourself?

Is there a conflicting truth in that lie – something that is true when you look at it through the lens of the gospel?

How does a conflicting truth help you see a different perspective of yourself or God and His work in your life?

Walking Out Revelation

Do not merely listen to the word, and so deceive yourselves.
Do what it says. Anyone who listens to the word but
does not do what it says is like someone who looks at his
face in a mirror and, after looking at himself, goes away
and immediately forgets what he looks like. But whoever
looks intently into the perfect law that gives freedom,
and continues in it—not forgetting what they have heard,
but doing it—they will be blessed in what they do.

James 1:22-25 (NIV)

I love being practical. Don't you? I mean I love being inspired and having my heart and my mind motivated and challenged to live the best life that I possibly can. But when I finish a book or listen to a message or teaching, I like two things: that I can relate, and it's relevant to me.

Practical steps to put into practice.

Revelation without application is just information. And too often we can hear or read a great and inspirational message and be encouraged and comforted in the moment. But then three days or a week later we have forgotten or we begin to doubt. It just doesn't seem to stick.

Now, 25 years into my journey with Christ and I can finally say I've learned a few tips about how to make things stick in my life. This can apply to anything. A bible reading plan, study, healthy eating and even exercise!

Plan: If we want to achieve anything in life, we need to be intentional. Having a good idea or intention is great. Walking it out is even better! What's that old saying? Words without actions are dead. So let's be intentional by setting aside a time each day. It can be as little as 5 or 10 minutes to start with. Put it in your calendar, make it a priority.

Preparation: Make a space, have what you need ready to go. Organize any other commitments around that time. Maybe it's when the kids are in bed or at school. When the hubs is happily snoring and your phone is switched to silent. But like we used to say in Girl Guides. (the Aussie version of Girl Scouts). Be prepared!

Purpose: Know the purpose behind what you're going after. Write it down.

Proverbs 29:18 says 'Without a vision people go astray'. In other words know and remind yourself what the WHY is behind the what and the how. For example we have a new puppy, Kevin. Our vision for him is to be an obedient and well behaved dog. Our 'How' is to take him on a walk in the morning. Why? Because if he doesn't get enough attention and exercise, he eats our furniture! The sacrifice of rolling out of bed to walk the dog even when we don't feel like it, is worth it!

Perseverance: Technically it takes 63 days for the brain to build new synapses and pathways for something you believe to become truth. That is an actual neurological fact. So whether it's a new habit you are trying to establish, or a new mindset or belief system, remember that it takes time.

Posture: Posture your heart to receive from God. You have made the space, you have prepared and you know the end goal. So come in expectation and faith, to receive what you are believing for. This can apply to anything. Your devotion time, when you're creating or building something, exercise and even rest.

Partner: We are spiritual beings living in a physical body. So we have the opportunity to partner with God in everything we do. He is my writing muse, my exercise buddy, my business partner, my counselor, and my best cheerleader. I include him in everything I do. And when we do, he orders our steps along the way.

Process: Record your process. Remind yourself of your why. Write down your ideas, thoughts and revelation and meditate over it. As you process with the Holy Spirit, you will see progress in what you're doing.

Progress: Another word for this is momentum. There is a momentum that starts to build as you continue to intentionally process what you're going after. And as you reflect on that, you progressively move forward.

Promise: There is power in his promises. Make sure that you not only have your vision and purpose before you, but remind yourself of the promises that he has for you in what you are going after. Write them down, declare them, pray through them, pursue them and speak them out over what you are believing God for.

Peace: Rest in him. Rest in the knowledge that there is grace for you in this season. Whether it's just five minutes in the shower, or 15 minutes folding the laundry. If it's in the car on the way to work or early in the morning before the world awakes. His grace empowers you for the season you're in and brings with it, the peace that passes all understanding as you rest in him.

I'm quite sure there are more. But 10 'P's' are more than enough for today. Be encouraged my friend, God is with you every step of the way! Let's be women of purpose, doers of the Word and not just hearers only.! And as we step out we will be blessed in everything we do.

Author: Kim Beaumont

REFLECTION QUESTIONS

What are some tips you can add to this list that work for you?

What is one step you could take today that could help you put into practice what you are pursuing?

Stuck in the Muck

I waited patiently for the Lord;
He turned to me and heard my cry.
He lifted me out of the slimy pit,
out of the mud and mire;
He set my feet on a rock
and gave me a firm place to stand.

Psalm 40:1-2 (NIV)

G rowing up on a ranch, one thing I dreaded was what we called "muck": that deep, stinky, miry mixture of manure and mud that globs onto boots and clothing in the springtime. Not only would it cover everything, but sometimes we'd really get our feet stuck in it. Every so often my brothers and I would be walking through the corrals to do chores, unsuspecting of the suction capacity that the muck had, and suddenly find ourselves with our "muck boots" ...and sometimes our socks...sucked right off of our feet before we realized that we were standing in that slimy, smelly muck in our bare feet!

I remember one day the boys and I watching as our mother attempted to cross the quagmire of the corral and stepped right on out of her muck boots. As she tried to pull her feet out, she lost her balance and fell down smack dab in the middle of the muck! My brothers and I looked at one another with huge eyes, wondering how she was going to handle this dilemma and if there would be tears and angry words.

We were prepared for a full-on meltdown. After all, there my mother was, sitting in about six inches of manurey mud, covered from head to toe in it. Each time she would stick her hands down to attempt to push herself up and out, she would end up falling back in. The more she tried to get out of the sticky situation, the more covered in muck she became! She finally looked up at us kids and said, "Guys, I could sit here and wallow in this muck, feeling sorry for myself, angry at everyone and frustrated for the predicament I'm in... or you three could come down off of the fence, get in the muck with me, and pull me out!" Until we got down in the middle of the yuck with her, she was left helplessly stuck.

Sometimes isn't that just like life? We're going about our days, unsuspecting and probably enjoying the sunshine on our face, a soft breeze in our hair, loved ones surrounding us, accomplishing the work God has set before us, when suddenly we find ourselves facing a situation that has us mired down and stuck. The death of a loved one, problems in our marriage, a job loss, financial insecurity, health issues, prodigal children, aging parents, among a myriad of other reasons that we become stuck in the miry clay of circumstances. Feeling defeated, discouraged, and stuck, not really knowing how to get out of the mess we're sitting in the middle of.

It stinks (sometimes literally it literally stinks) when we find ourselves in these situations that keep us stuck. And just like my mother, we have two choices: Continue to sit there in the muck and mire, feeling sorry for ourselves, or look for help to get out of it. I have learned so many times that deliverance comes when we look to the Lord for rescue from the slimy pit of mud and mire, those things in life that trip us up, and leave us feeling vulnerable and stuck.

Trust me, God wants us stuck even less than we want to be stuck! He has a plan and a purpose for our lives, plans to give us peace and not evil, a future and a hope (Jeremiah 29:11, NKJV). He wants us to be effective and active in the work that He has called us to; being stuck in the mud and manure of life keeps us from doing that work.

Another memory that sticks out to me is when I was in college. After failing my freshman year and finding myself on academic probation, I sunk into a miry pit of depression, anxiety, discouragement and shame. I walked out to a huge boulder that sat in the middle of one of our pastures, climbed up onto it and cried out to the Lord. Gut wrenching, soul deep crying. Just like He did with David, the Lord inclined to me. He heard my cries, brought me up out of that horrible pit I had put myself into, reached down and helped me stand up out of the miry muck. God cleaned me up, set me back on my feet; and in love, with grace and mercy He put a new song of praise in my mouth. If you ever find yourself stuck in a mucky pit of discouragement, shame, or trials, cry out to God. He hears and will rescue you.

Author: Jana Fraley

REFLECTION QUESTIONS

Have you ever felt stuck because of grief, disappointment, discouragement or shame?

Did you try and get "unstuck" on your own, how did that work?

Have you ever experienced God reaching down and pulling you out of a pit of your own making?

Facing Uncertainty with God

Preserve me, O God, for in you I take refuge.
I say to the LORD, "You are my Lord;
I have no good apart from you.

You make known to me the path of life;
in your presence there is fullness of joy;
at your right hand are pleasures forevermore.

Psalm 16:1-2, 11 (ESV)

I t was 1973. I was in Madison, Wisconsin visiting a high school friend after having attended a missionary convention in Illinois. This friend and I had in our younger years shared many crazy experiences with drugs, anti-war protests, and racing each other to see who could lose their virginity first. My freshman year of college continued that trend as I let go of all restraint and gave myself to doing whatever was "right in my own eyes." At the end, I was wasted emotionally and physically and because of it, God began to prepare my heart to receive Him, which I did in a dramatic turn of events in the fall of 1972.

Now it is 1973 and I am staying with the same friend in Wisconsin whose life has not changed direction. She has continued going on into more destructive paths. She and I are trying to navigate our friendship, but it is becoming clear that we are operating in two different worlds with very different philosophies. The missionary convention I attended was amazing. I did not grow up in a Christian family and everything about my faith was new to me. I was now part of this new group of people who were very straight-laced and conservative. And while I was struggling to understand where I fit in, there was something very stable and secure about this new community. I loved the Bible and loved learning about the Bible. Growing up as a secular Jewish person had not given me any connection with the Bible. We had recited the 23rd Psalm in elementary school and I had read the book of Jonah for an English class in high school but other than that, I had never cracked a Bible! Now I was devouring the Bible every day, couldn't get enough of it, and through my reading, God was beginning to change my heart from the inside out.

During this visit, my friend had tried by any means to draw me back into the worldly lifestyle we had experienced together. I resisted but felt so unsure of myself. It was time for me to head back to college in New York and I was feeling very anxious about all the changes that had come into my life and how I was going to handle them. I visited a Christian bookstore and purchased an album of worship songs that were all based on Scripture. My friend was at work and I put the album on her stereo and listened to a song called, "You Are My God."[1] It was taken from Psalm 16 and the words and music drew me in. The singer sang out, "You are my God, you alone are my joy, defend me, O God!" I played the song over and over, lifting my hands up to God, placing my whole life, all future decisions, all unforeseen difficulties, all my insecurities into His hands. It was my own personal dedication to God. I realized God was truly with me and was going to be with me throughout my life. I sang the last verse of the song with joy and triumph: "You show me the path of my life, in your presence the fullness of joy, to be at your right hand forever, for me would be happiness always." I was going back to college with all of its challenges and uncertainties, but I was going with God.

Author: Miriam Kook

REFLECTION QUESTIONS

How do you help yourself when you are on the precipice of uncertainty?

What Scripture verses do you look to for comfort and encouragement when needed?

Drowning in Mercy

Then Peter came to him and asked, 'Lord, how often should I forgive someone who sins against me? Seven times?' 'No, not seven time,' Jesus replied, 'but seventy times seven!'

Matthew 18:21-22 (NLT)

Mercy is defined as compassion or forgiveness shown toward someone who has the power to punish or harm another.

There was a person who had a great debt owed, far greater than their ability to pay, even in their total lifetime of working. The one to whom the debt was owed had power enough to severely punish this person until the great debt was fully paid. Instead, mercy was extended. Mercy holds nothing back if the debt was paid, it was fully cancelled, just like that.

That same person, with a newly clean slate, then left and though most would be leaping for joy at the paid off debt, instead with a different agenda, he came to another man. Taking hold of him by the neck, the released one shook and screamed asking for the debt that this fellow man owed him. See, though much had been forgiven and cancelled for the one, he still had a small debt owed to him. A debt that could barely compare to the one that he, himself had been released from just earlier. Yet, here he was, choking it out of this poor sap.

Clearly choking them was not going to squeeze it out of him.

Yet I spent far too long living as this released person. Having come to the Lord in surrender and being fully forgiven as 1 John 1:9 says. The One who had seen my darkest sin had fully covered it by His blood. Released. Completely. Tremendous debt, paid in full.

And yet, I have held the neck of my dear husband begging him for the debt, that in my eyes, he owed me. He had wronged me. Never mind that I had wronged him as well. Two sinners in one marriage, it happens, often. We argue, or at best, disagree. Then we claim to forgive; yet, we carry the legal pad of wrongs tucked under our arm waiting for the next infraction so that we might be quick to pounce and demand repayment.

I have done this by bringing up old infractions when we argue, or "punishing" him with the silent treatment, or not being the first to apologize.

I have withheld real, complete, and total forgiveness from him and from others too. When the reality is that by the great mercy of God, I have been released from an eternal debt I could never repay.

I am drowning in mercy. So how is it I withhold mercy from others?

If we possess an ocean of forgiving waters, why must we be stingy with a cup of it?

Author: Mariel Davenport

REFLECTION QUESTIONS

Have you acknowledged your own need for forgiveness of your great debt of sin and sought the only One, Jesus Christ, who has the power to offer you the mercy you need?

Who are you still choking for the cup of water worth of debt? A parent, sibling, spouse, friend? They might have hurt you, wrong you, abandon you. But that is a mere cup of water in comparison with the ocean of mercy the Lord Jesus offers us.

How can you release them today to the One who judges justly? (1 Peter 2:21-23)

Finding Home

Jesus answered him, 'If anyone loves me, he will keep
my word, and my Father will love him, and we will
come to him and we will make our home with him.'

John 14:23 (ESV)

It happened in the fourth grade. I came through the school doors at recess
time and saw my friends, a short distance away, standing in a huddle. As
I waved and walked toward them, they saw me and ran away. Confused,
I thought they were playing a game. I spent the entire recess time looking,
spotting, running after them as they ran away from me. Grade 4 girl-games
are not very funny.

Back in the classroom I told them, "Guys, that wasn't funny!" Side glances.
They said nothing.

The same thing happened the next day. And the next. Finally, I caught up
with them, waiting at the door to go in.

"Look!" she said, hand on hip, eyes on mine, "We just don't want you
here, okay?!"

And in that moment, somewhere deep inside, her words wrote on a name
tag and pierced it to my heart: *"Outsider."*

I had lived there, in that little town, for two years, and for the first little
while I was a novelty to a group of kids who had grown up next door to
grandparents and cousins. Everyone wanted to talk to the "new girl" who
had "come from away." I had never had trouble making friends before, and
this new adventure, this quaint little town was no exception. *Until that day.* I
supposed that two years was the amount of time it took to tell the new-com-
er that she will never belong. She might live here now, but it's not her *home.*

That name tag stayed with me all the rest of my growing up years. Through new friendships that came and went. Through seasons and change, different schools, different houses, different towns. Even different provinces. My search for home and belonging became elusive. A feather in the wind, painfully close, but forever just out of reach.

I think of Mary and Joseph, all those years ago, desperate to find a place to deliver their tiny treasure, God made flesh. I imagine how they must have felt, slamming door after slamming door as Mary's contractions grew closer and closer together.

Arms around his wailing wife, hands gripped by hers, I wonder if Joseph looked at the warm candlelight glowing from windows of those who had found a place to belong, and felt the deep ache for home.

But these beautiful outsiders were about to hold the only home they would ever need, and not just for them, but for any and all who would behold Him and believe Him.

Years later, my husband and I took our children on a trip back to my little home-but-not-hometown where I did most of my growing up. By now my *Outsider* name tag had become a jagged thorn, lodged in my heart, soul bleeding out. Retracing my steps, I hoped that if I could revisit the place where the door first slammed shut for *me,* maybe I could find what I couldn't see before, my missing piece. A quiet corner in this little town where I could find my own tiny treasure, my sense of home, in the place where I'd first lost it.

I wish I could tell you that I found it there, this missing piece, this feeling of home, but I didn't. It was months later before I realized that finding everything the same and yet profoundly different made me realize that I had traveled 2,000 miles to find something I'd already had since my wide-eyed wonder at the age of four, when Jesus became the treasure of my heart. *Emmanuel.* God *with* me. God *within* me.

Home is not a *place.* Home is a *person. And His name is Jesus.*

Author: Jennifer Hayes

REFLECTION QUESTIONS

What feelings does the word "home" bring up in you?

What are some of the ways you have looked for that "home" feeling in the past?   Did it work? Why or why not?

What does it mean to you to know that "home" can only truly be found in the presence of Jesus? How does this change how you see yourself and/or your circumstances?

There's a Donut Shop

'Bring the whole tithe into the store-house. Then there will be food in My House. Now test Me in this' says Adonai -TZva'ot '- if I will not open for you the windows of heaven, and pour out blessing for you, until no one is without enough.'

Malachi 3:10 (TLV)

"Mommy, please can we get donuts on the way to church? We are so hungry," my nine-year-old daughter exclaimed from the back seat. My two-year old son pleaded with his eyes, eagerly agreeing to anything his big sister said. "I'm sorry kids," I replied. "Mommy doesn't have any extra money for donuts today. Besides, you already had cereal at our friends house this morning." "But Mom, I didn't really like that cereal and I'm still hungry! Please Mom! Look! There is a donut shop right next to the gas station. We can stop there," my daughter eagerly pleaded. How convenient, I thought to myself. "There's a donut shop right there," while sarcastically rolling my eyes. That strategically located donut shop was not helping my argument at all. But the kids were hungry and I knew they were, because neither one had hardly touched their cereal this morning.

You see, we were staying at the home of some people from the church we had just started attending. I was separated from my current husband and in the process of a divorce. We were literally living out of suitcases because I had left an abusive situation very quickly. I had made some poor choices too during the breakup, but I was trying to do the right things and get my act together. The kids and I were going to church and staying with this family, even though my current boyfriend was pressuring me to move in with him. We had counselled with our pastor and he strongly advised against living together and I knew he was right, even though things would be so much easier on me if I relented and moved in with this guy. I had no money saved to rent a place of my own and I could not go to any of our former friends or my soon to be ex-husband's family for help. I had no relatives of my own in this entire state we lived in, so we were truly on our own except for our new-found church family.

The pleading continued as I sat in the parking lot outside the donut shop. "What do I do God, what do I do?" I whispered to myself. I looked in my purse and spied that sealed white envelope. The one that had my tithe in it, in cash, the very first tithe that I had ever set aside to pay. That little voice in my head mocked me, reminded me of my choices, criticized me for even thinking that I could afford to pay a tithe and punched me in the gut with a swift jab at what a terrible mother I was, letting my kids go hungry. "Just take money out of that envelope for donuts. No one will ever know," the voice said. "But I will know, and God will know," I replied to that taunting voice.

Then another voice, this one gentler and kinder, whispered to me. "Look in your wallet again, just try one more time." So, I began looking in every nook and cranny and hiding spot in my wallet. To my amazement, I soon found a folded five-dollar bill stuck away. I pulled it out, giving God thanks as I happily told my children that we could get donuts after all. God had provided a way and my faithfulness to keep my tithe intact was rewarded. It might seem like such a small thing, a five-dollar bill and donuts for your kids. But to a baby believer and a new tither, it was a sign that God would provide for us, no matter what!

Author: Anita Stafford

REFLECTION QUESTIONS

Are you a regular tither? If not, why?

Have you ever been in a position where you had to make a difficult choice about whether to tithe or pay something else? What did you do?

How has God shown you that He will reward your faithfulness in tithing and giving at your church?

He Helps Us Find Our Lost Things

Faith is the assurance of things hoped for,
the conviction of things not seen.

Hebrews 11:1 (ESV)

F aith is my soul's response to a deep-rooted relationship with Abba. My faith has not been a rote response to becoming redeemed. It goes hand in hand with quality time spent reading the Word, praying both small, seemingly insignificant prayers and large, life-changing prayers.

Times when I have felt timid, unsure, and unsettled have been related to my lack of attention to those areas. When my heart is restless and my mind is easily distracted, I tend to wander away from the practices that are the building blocks to my relationship with God. In times of stress, God far too often becomes a part of my emergency rations.

Knowing God as my Abba has also been a slow growing process related to time spent with Him, not seeking an answer to a need, but relishing in His presence in worship or simply reading and scribing the Word, like nails being driven deep into the recesses of my soul. The nails become the pegs I can hang my troubles on. Each moment spent studying His character, praising His faithfulness, savoring His miracles, is an opportunity for these pegs to grow in fortitude, firmly planted in my soul.

Faith is often compared to a child, and when I consider my own five children, I know that unless they can come to trust my character and know my heart and deep love for them, their faith in my role as their mother will not stand the test of trials. Well-loved children, like that of Abba, know their parents love is genuine, and can come to trust that, even when being corrected, their love will stand the test of time.

When my oldest daughter was 3 years old, she lost a treasured toy. We searched in vain for "cheese" for days on end, scouring every nook and cranny, retracing our steps, and searching again, only to come up empty-handed. One evening, my husband and I were preparing ourselves to have the talk we had been avoiding for days, that beloved "cheese" was probably never going to be found. Just before telling our troubled toddler this news, he asked if we had even prayed for "cheese" to be found. In all honesty, I thought about it multiple times over the course of these days, but because my relationship was not firmly rooted on the character of God and His Word ("Rejoice always, pray without ceasing…" 1 Thessalonians 5:16-18 ESV), I saw my small prayer for "cheese" as an annoyance rather than an opportunity to talk to my Abba about something that was heavy on my heart. Honestly, have you ever berated a child for asking you for help in finding their lost lovey? Of course not. Relationships give us courage to trust. The deeper the connection, communion, and conversation, the deeper our ability to trust.

Kneeling there in our living room with our 3-year-old daughter, I was convicted, and that moment was the catalyst for deeper connection with my Abba as we stopped and prayed for His help in finding her lost "cheese." With a resounding Amen, the three of us began to stand up preparing for another hunt, when my husband heard in his spirit to look, yet again, under the couch. And there, not a few inches from the edge of the couch was the long sought-after lovey. We literally yelled, "No way!!!"

God does care about every little detail of our lives because He is our Abba. He wants to be included in our day, and when we pray without ceasing, we invite Him into the dishwashing, toothbrushing, vacuuming, meal planning, scheduling, conferences, carpooling, employee evaluations, grocery shopping, "cheese" hunting moments.

When our faith is wrapped up in our understanding of His great love for us, everything matters. Bring it all to Him because He cares about it all.

Author: Kristin Cash

REFLECTION QUESTIONS

When was a time you trusted God for something small and He showed up?

Do you ever feel that God is annoyed by the little details of your life?

If you do not have a healthy relationship with your earthly father, what are some ways you can begin to develop a stronger connection to God as your Abba?

Living & Active

For the word of God is living and active.

Hebrews 4:12 (NIV)

In the fall of 2019, I was working through a Beth Moore Bible study and one of the verses that stood out to me was, "And we have come to know and to believe the love God has for us" 1 John 4:16a (CSB). I recognized immediately that I wanted this to be true in my life. I wanted to know the love that God has for us as fully as I could. I wanted to believe the love of God completely. This verse became my prayer and over the next few months, God taught me more about His love. One thing He used was a sermon by Tim Keller called, "Struggle: Thy Will Be Done." This is an excellent sermon which focuses on Jesus' struggle in the Garden of Gethsemane. Keller asks a question that I had never considered in all the times I have read the various passages on this scene. Why did Jesus suddenly become sorrowful and troubled in the garden? He had been talking about His death for weeks and suddenly it was troubling Him. Keller believes that Jesus had begun to experience what was to come on the cross—complete separation from the Father. He would, for the first time, be cut off from the presence of the rest of the Trinity. He would experience something that none of us would ever have to face because of what He was doing—the Father's rejection. As Jesus began to experience what He would fully suffer the next day, He wanted another solution. He wanted the Father to find another way. He wrestled and prayed and then He surrendered to the Father's will. As I came to understand more of what Jesus felt in the garden, His surrender to the cost He would have to pay tore my heart. I knew He did it because of His love for us. And I had a new understanding of the depth of His love. God used that sermon to help me to know and to believe the love He has for us. That verse in the CSB version had become a prayer that strengthened my faith in a powerful way.

But God wasn't done with showing me truth through that verse. The other day I had pulled out some old journals and was reading one from the summer of 2011. I discovered an entry in which I quoted, "And so we know and rely on the love God has for us" 1 John 4:16a (NIV). I was asking God to fill me with so much love that it flowed out of my life to those around me. I wrote, "I am relying on the love You have for me. I know that it will not fail because it is unshakeable." I was recognizing walls that I had placed in my heart, fear that kept me trapped behind those walls. God was showing me that it was His love that could help tear down those walls and drive out the fear I had. As I read through more entries in the journal from 2011, I found another one that quotes this verse again as I continued to write about the fear I was feeling at the time. I wrote, "The verses preceding 1 John 4:16a speak of what God has done that shows His love for us—that He sent His Son as Savior of the world. Such a simple statement, that we accept as true, and yet we rarely think about all that this truth involves. I cling to my fear, focus on my pain and loneliness, and disregard all that You did to show Your love for me."

As I read those entries from 2011, I was struck by how God had used the same verse, several years apart, from two different versions, to teach me about His love. It was the same truth throughout, but He taught me more each time. And even today as I wrote out the last quote from my journal, I saw more of that truth. "Such a simple statement, that we accept as true, and yet we rarely think about all that this truth involves." I wrote that in 2011 and several years later God used a sermon by Tim Keller to impress upon me more of "all that this truth involves." The verse that came to mind as I pondered these things was the one from Hebrews saying that God's Word is living and active. I love that about Scripture. And I love that God continues to teach me the same truths from different angles so that I understand more fully the truths He wants me to know. As I more fully know truth, I more fully know Him. And I want to know Him as fully and completely as I can!

Author: Barb Loewen

REFLECTION QUESTIONS

What Scriptures has God used to teach you more of the same truth but at different times?

How have you experienced the word of God as living and active in your life?

In what way has God helped you to know and to believe the love He has for us or to know and rely on that love?

The Power of Declaration

For as the rain and snow came down from the heavens, and
return not there again, but water the earth and make it spring
forth and sprout, that it may give seed to the sower and bread
to the eater. So shall my word be that which goes forth out of
my mouth: it shall not return to Me void (without producing
any effect, useless) but it shall accomplish that which I please
and purpose, and it shall prosper in the thing for which I sent it.

Isaiah 55:10-11 (AMPC)

I love a good challenge, don't you? A few years ago I decided to join a 40 day declaration challenge. The aim - to daily declare God's promises over different areas of our lives. Intentionality is one of my 'things'. So I grabbed a journal and started literally listing all the declarations and promises of God I could think of. Being a 'list girl' is another one of my things. So I began and busily started listing. I was ready! Little did I know the impact the next 40 days would have on me.

Each day I would pull out my journal and go through my list, reciting and declaring his promises. Counting them as I went. Determined to finish my list. Day one, two, three passed. Still going strong. Day four, five and six still faithfully reciting my list. Day seven, eight, nine, my enthusiasm started to wane, but I plodded along. Now I'm just being real here. For some of you by now I'm sure you probably would have memorized a book of the bible, experienced angelic visitations, or at the very least encountered the sweet intimate presence of the Lord. But for me, nothing. Zip! But sometimes we just need to stick to the last thing that God asked us to do until he says otherwise? No matter the feelings, expectations or doubts that may be trying to sway us otherwise. So onwards I plodded. If nothing else, I could still be obedient.

Religiously I listed those declarations day in and day out, now beginning to know them by heart. Determined to finish this challenge, I walked, cleaned the house, drove my car, grocery shopped, washed my hair while uttering my list faithfully every day. I can still remember walking down our dusty country road with my dog Jazz and quietly listing on my fingers the declarations as I went through them.

Day 30 arrived, and something finally started to shift. I began to realize that as I prayed and declared these simple truths over and over I would be prompted and reminded of something or someone as I recited a specific promise or scripture. And as I followed the thought I would begin to pray for that person or situation with a fervor and a heart for them that I had never experienced before. I could literally feel God's heart for that particular situation. I would pray until the conviction ceased and then continue to my next declaration. My prayer life exploded!

I began to look forward more and more to our walks each day. The connection between God and myself grew deep and grew strong. And as I quietly listed my declarations on my fingers as I walked, and spoke those promises over my children, our business, my fears and dreams, Jesus walked alongside of me. Whispering to my heart, ministering to my soul and increasing my love and value for him and the power of his word.

Just like his promise in 2 Corinthians 9:10-11, his word watered me with his presence, bringing seed to the sower, as I continued to faithfully sow one declaration at a time. And he bought bread to the eater, as I feasted on those promises that exploded in my heart.

Even as I write this, there is a warmth and affection as I remember what he did in my heart in that season. Not only was it a beautiful precious time with him. But he established in me a revelation of the power of his word that increases as we partner with him and declare OUT LOUD his promises. Prayers were answered yes, but it was even more than that! The door was opened even wider, giving me even greater access to him. I can't even put into words what that is like. And I remember it to this day.

So I want to encourage you today. He is there just waiting with open arms for you to step out, be obedient and open your mouth. And as you begin to declare his promises over your life, those words will not return void or empty, but accomplish what they are sent out to do. And even more than you could ever hope, dream or imagine.

Author: Kim Beaumont

REFLECTION QUESTIONS

Write out three of your favorite promises over your life.

Why are they so special to you?

What areas in your life right now need some of God's promises declared over them?

Foot in Mouth Disease

He who guards his mouth preserves his life, but he
who opens wide his lips shall have destruction.

Proverbs 13:3 (NKJV)

There's a nasty virus that hits livestock called "Foot and Mouth Disease". It hasn't shown up in the United States for almost a hundred years, but it got me thinking about a different kind of foot and mouth disease that I have to inoculate against, and it's called "Foot In Mouth Disease"; meaning open mouth, insert foot!

I remember when I was about 13 years old and at 4-H camp. My mother was one of the chaperones at camp and I overheard some kids making fun of her, laughing at the fact that she had a dead front tooth that was greyish brown from falling off a bed when she was a child. Mom was always paranoid about that tooth, but it never really bothered me because it was just a part of who she was. That day, though, listening to those kids make fun of my mother and her tooth, I became embarrassed and paranoid about it as well. I was mad, not at the kids who were being cruel, but angry at my mom. I found her in our cabin and sharply lashed out, "Mom! A bunch of kids are talking about your tooth! Why can't you fix that stupid, ugly black tooth?!" The moment the words were out of my mouth I was filled with remorse and regret; but rather than apologize, I burst into tears and ran off, leaving my mother standing there in shock at my outburst.

I wish I could say this was the one and only time I ever dealt with this dreaded disease, but it was just one instance out of many that I have said words I wanted to take back. It takes a lifetime to build up an immunity to this destructive virus, and it's taken God showing me time and again that the words I speak have the ability to hurt or to heal. It's a lesson that has been particularly difficult to learn as a mother and a wife. I cringe when I think about words spoken in the heat of anger, impatience, frustration, or fear; words that cut my loved ones to the quick. Or words said about others that weren't my words to speak, words that were nothing more than gossip dressed up fancy to look like concern or "prayer requests", words that had the potential to cause deep hurt to the one they were spoken about.

Through the years I've struggled with saying too many words that have no value or benefit to myself or the one listening to me. Silent pauses have always made me feel uncomfortable, and I fight the temptation to fill the silence with unnecessary talk. Sometimes it's nothing more than "empty calories", they sound good, but carry no nutritional value. Sometimes my words are like actual poison, where the intent is to harm the one hearing them.

Proverbs 16:23-24 (NKJV) says, "The heart of the wise teaches his mouth, and adds learning to his lips. Pleasant words are like a honeycomb, sweetness to the soul and health to the bones." The words I speak and how I control them reflect what wisdom my heart holds. A sure sign of a wise woman is whether she has learned how to control the words she speaks. Our words have such power! The power to bring pleasantness and blessing, life, and health. Our words also have the power to bring horrible destruction and harm. Just a couple chapters later in Proverbs 18:6-7,21 (NKJV) we're told, "A fool's lips enter into contention, and his mouth calls for blows. A fool's mouth is his destruction, and his lips are the snare of his soul...Death and life are in the power of the tongue."

My tongue holds power for the greatest good and the greatest harm. James 3:5,6,8 (NKJV) says, "See how great a forest a little fire kindles! And the tongue is a fire, a world of iniquity... But no man can tame the tongue. It is an unruly evil, full of deadly poison." The key to using my tongue for good and not evil lies in controlling it; but since "no man can tame the tongue", I recognize that God's power is the only thing that can keep my tongue from wagging out of control, causing hurt and destruction.

I have come to discover the only remedy for this disease is a humble surrender of my heart and my mouth to the Lord so that He can set a guard over it, making the words of my mouth and the meditation of my heart acceptable in His sight (Psalm 19:14, NKJV). I want my words to build and encourage, not destroy, and discourage.

Author: Jana Fraley

REFLECTION QUESTIONS

Has there been an instance where "Foot in Mouth Disease" has gotten you in trouble or hurt someone else?

How has God helped you in keeping your words "acceptable in His sight?"

When have the words spoken by another been beneficial and encouraging in your life?

Like Newborn Babes

But I have calmed and quieted my soul,
like a weaned child with its mother;
like a weaned child is my soul within me.

Psalm 131:2 (ESV)

Like newborn infants, long for the pure spiritual
milk, that by it you may grow up into salvation

1 Peter 2:2 (ESV)

I loved nursing my babies. It was one time in my young life when I wasn't frantically running around, trying to prove I was someone. And I recall that my babies loved nursing too. I laughingly remember when I would put them in the feeding position while I was trying to unhook my nursing bra, they would hyperventilate in stress and anticipation. I would hurry as fast as I could, saying, "Okay, it's coming, it's coming!!" Then when they finally latched on, the trembling would stop, and in its place, extreme calm. We would both settle in for a precious few minutes of peace and oxytocin.

Peter tells us that in this same way, like hungry babies, we should greatly long for and earnestly desire the pure spiritual milk of the Word. What makes us develop such a frantic desire? It comes from having already tasted this pure, spiritual milk and from the memory of how it affected us in that God's lovingkindness washed over our souls, cleansing us, and setting us free from all that held us captive. And when we inevitably get thirsty again, we want to experience more of this love, of this revelation, of this freedom! In discovering God's kindness when we read the Bible, we get hooked on the joy of having God speak to us. His words to us are so encouraging and life-changing. Very different from the way the world speaks to us. The more we drink, the more we desire it.

Some people talk about "first love," a love for God and His Word that kind of intoxicates new believers and swaddles them close to Him, kind of like the way a mother keeps her newborn baby close to her. John in the book of Revelation talks about the possibility of losing our first love. If we can lose it, we can also keep and grow it, by stimulating it. I remember feeling this first love when I had just become a believer when I was in college. I was so aware of Jesus' presence and person that I thought He was going to come back to earth any minute. I went to visit my mom one weekend and when I returned to school, I accidentally left my Bible at her house. I called her crying, asking her to please go right out and mail my Bible to me. I had to wait three days for it to arrive and when it did, I was like my hyperventilating baby, tearing the paper off the mailer, releasing my Bible, and hugging it to myself. Look how precious it was to me. When Corrie and Betsie ten Boom, two Dutch sisters who had hidden Jews from the Nazis during World War II, were caught, and were imprisoned in a concentration camp, they risked death by smuggling a Bible in with them and it became the most precious object to many of the women in their barracks.

What if we never felt this hyperventilating need for the Word? What if we tried and it didn't seem to speak to us? Even some babies struggle to latch on or drink for longer than a couple of minutes at a time. But it is still important for them to learn to drink in order to thrive. So, maybe we drink in short spurts, maybe we get creative in how we read. Figure out what touches you. Read a little, journal a little, listen to some Scripture in music, draw pictures or paint Bible stories or quotes. Maybe try a new translation, or get a study Bible with helpful notes, listen to the Bible online rather than read, or read a children's Bible storybook or watch a Bible movie. I really dislike winter. Between October 20-March 20 (the end of winter) there are 150 days. I start reading Psalms backwards. I start with Psalm 150 and the next day Psalm 149, etc. Every day, I am closer to winter being over and this makes me happy. (I know this sounds crazy, but this is how I motivate myself to read and besides, the Psalms are wonderful!) Try to find your own quirky ways of reading. Keep trying, pray for God to help you develop a taste for His kindness.

Author: Miriam Kook

REFLECTION QUESTIONS

How do you feel about reading the Bible?

What verse(s) in the Bible have spoken of God's kindness and love to you?

Pick a book of the Bible to read through. Make note of every reference to God's lovingkindness towards people and apply those words of lovingkindness to yourself.

Remaining in the Hard Places

Pray also for me, that whenever I speak, words
may be given me so that I will fearlessly make
known the mystery of the gospel.

Ephesians 6:19 (NIV)

I have been in a marriage I wanted out of, even planned to leave. By God's stunning and undeserved grace, I stayed, so did my husband. But before you read that too fast, please know that getting from then until now in our marriage has been a long, hard, and ugly road.

How is it that my husband and I stayed when our hearts wanted out? How is it that anyone stays when the desire to run overtakes them? Not only from an unstable marriage, but even from that which we have no real choice to run from, a health diagnosis, the pain of a wayward child, being caregiver to an elderly parent, or deep grief that hounds us. Life doesn't always afford us the luxury of packing up the old circumstances and picking new ones, in fact, rarely is that an option, if ever.

Paul knew this well, as he sat in prison writing to the church at Ephesus. He gives us a beautiful example of how to remain in the hard circumstances. He didn't just grin and bear it, far from it!

1. **He asked others to pray for him.** In Ephesians 6:19, he asks the believers he is writing to for prayer, not for his release, but for his boldness as he remains in the trial. His desire is to glorify God in and through it not just to run from it.

2. **He takes his eyes off himself.** When we find ourselves feeling stuck in a staying situation that is hard and requires endurance, we can easily send out pity-party invitations and wallow in our own self-pity. Not Paul, he writes this bold letter to the Ephesians to sharpen them and in verse 22 of chapter 6 he tells them he is sending his buddy, Tychicus, for the purpose of encouraging them. I have to think that he was encouraged himself as he took his eyes off his situation and instead looked to encourage others in theirs.

3. **He focuses on God's plan in the situation.** Why might the Lord have me here in this season? Nothing is in vain in the Lord's economy, so there is purpose in and for every season under Heaven. Paul recognizes that the Lord can use *even this* for His glory. So rather than looking at his own desire to run from the circumstance, he looks to boldly proclaiming the mystery of the gospel right there in the middle of that hard place.

My husband and I eventually got to the place of looking towards God's purpose, praying for God's Will and seeking to please the Lord with our marriage. By His grace, we are now in our second decade of marriage. Hard circumstances don't always end that way, regardless of the ending, the purpose is always for us to grow in our walk with the Lord and know Him better. When we follow Paul's example, the ending always works together for the good of those called according to His purpose (Romans 8:28), whether we see it here or in Glory.

Author: Mariel Davenport

REFLECTION QUESTIONS

What about us? How might we then be like Paul, in the inevitable hard places we find ourselves? Who have you asked to pray for you in it?

Is your focus on seeking what God's good purpose might be and how you can be a light for those around you right where you are?

Freedom in Fences

From one man he made all the nations, that they should inhabit the whole earth; and he marked out their appointed times in history and the boundaries of their lands.

Acts 17:26 (NIV)

I've always been a girl who liked rules. Clear expectations and boundaries made me feel safe. I liked knowing what was expected of me. For this little people-pleasing-approval-junkie, knowing exactly how to win affection and earn favor was both comforting and rewarding.

But somehow amid the balancing, respecting, and striving to meet the expectations of those around me, I believed the lie that having boundaries of my own was selfish, even *sinful,* and decidedly *un-Christlike.* Soon the needs of all people everywhere rested squarely on my frail little shoulders, the responsibility for their eternity in my fumbling little hands.

Then the shape of my own life began to change. I had three high-needs children that required so much more of me than I had to give. My own health began to decline. These new, frustrating limitations were preventing me from being all things to all people. I began to resent my circumstances, my commitments, my children, my own body. I held these limitations as the enemy, the immovable barrier to my ability to love, serve, and worship. I was failing, and as failure gave way to fear, it gobbled up my peace and spewed out anxiety. The harder I tried to be "like Jesus," the less I resembled Him, and the farther away grace seemed to slip.

Learning the art of self-care and boundary building took a finesse that I just didn't seem to have. Intellectually, I understood the importance of it, but I just couldn't seem to get my heart around it. Stripping down my calendar, forcing myself to rest, spending money and time, making appointments and commitments for myself and my wellness...it all just felt so *selfish*.

Then I had a series of "a-ha" moments, beginning with a story in Simply Tuesday by Emily P. Freeman where she described a trip to the community pool with her children. While her kids swam and she lounged on a recliner close by, she noticed the strategic placement and purposeful demeanor of the lifeguards every 8 feet around the pool. They each stood guard over their own 8 ft. section, attentive, alert, focused. They were not distracted or concerned with what was happening in the other sections of the pool. They were diligently keeping watch *only over their own section*.

A short time later, while reading through the book of Acts, this one verse jumped off the page:

> "From one man he made all the nations, that they should inhabit the whole earth; and he marked out their appointed times in history and *the boundaries of their lands*" (Acts 17:26, italics mine).

As I let the implications of this verse clasp hands with Emily's story, I also remembered a research study a friend had mentioned to me. The study had found that children playing in *fenced in* playgrounds are more creative, carefree, and relaxed in their playing environment than children in wide-open play spaces with *no clear and visible boundaries*. Children in the wide-open playgrounds with no fences were less likely to play together and more likely to show signs of timidity, anxiety, and fear.

Like a slow sunrise, I felt this simple, but important truth finally wrapping itself around my heart. I had allowed my peace and joy to be swallowed up by the vast expanse of never-ending needs. I was perpetually depleted, chronically distracted, hopelessly exhausted. By trying to be everything to everyone, I found myself with nothing to offer anyone, most of all my own precious family; my own 8-foot stretch of territory.

But my ever-patient Savior gently corrected my relentless striving, my directionless chasing, my desperate hemorrhaging. I began to see my limitations in a new light, not as barriers, but as blessings. Not as sources of pain and angst, but catalysts for peace and joy, a release from responsibilities *that were never mine*. When we embrace the limitations that our good and kind Father has drawn for us, we can release the weight of responsibility for the things that are not ours to carry, the things that hunch our shoulders and buckle our knees. Then comes fresh air and freedom, permission, and purpose to say no to the very good things *intended for someone else,* so we can embrace the very *best* things that God has *intended for us.* Only then can we can tend and steward our own 8-foot territory well.

Author: Jennifer Hayes

REFLECTION QUESTIONS

What feelings/thoughts does the word *boundaries* bring up in you? Why do you think that is?

When you take the word *boundaries* to the Lord, what does He show you? What do you hear Him saying?

Can you name at least one limitation in your life that might actually be a boundary the Lord has drawn for you? What might this boundary be releasing you from?

Does this change how you respond to your circumstances? How?

The Word Hidden in My Heart

Bind them on your heart always; tie them around
your neck. When you walk, they will lead you;
when you lie down, they will watch over you; and
when you awake, they will talk with you.

Proverbs 6:21-22 (ESV)

I huddled on the bathroom floor with my back against the locked door. I sat in the dark and I was terrified. I did not know anything else to do or anywhere else to go. In my terror, all that I could do was repeat every Bible verse that I had ever helped my children memorize. A – All have sinned and come short of the glory of God. B – Believe on the Lord Jesus Christ and you shall be saved. C – Children, obey your parents in the Lord, for this is right. D – Depart from evil and do good. E – Even a child is known by his doings. F – Fear not for I am with you. My mind hung on that verse. Fear not for I am with you! When I could not remember any further, I started back at the beginning. A, B, C, D E, F and repeat. Occasionally, I would stop to listen. Was he still out there? What was he doing?

Who and what was I hiding from? My husband! He had told me before we got married that he was a recovered alcoholic, but now he had fallen off the wagon, and he had fallen hard. Not only was he drinking again, but he was doing drugs. That night he had come in from being out and when I awoke to find him at the edge of the bed, the face I saw looking back at me was not that of my husband, even though it was. There was an influence there that I can only recall now as demonic or other-worldly, certainly not the man that I had married. In my terror of the face that I saw gazing down at me, I had flown out of bed, locked myself in the bathroom, and now sat there in fear, repeating God's Word over and over, and over again.

When all seemed quiet for some time, I slowly and carefully crept out of the bathroom to find myself alone in the house again. Where he had gone or when he would be back, I did not know. It was not uncommon for him to be gone overnight or for several days at a time. For the time being, I was alone. Time would prove that he could not stay sober and clean and would eventually lead to the end of our marriage. But for now, I would learn to handle the cycles of sober and not-sober, clean, and unclean, all while sheltering and caring for our children, our home, and our business.

The Word that I had hidden in my heart, even though at the time it was an exercise in helping my children memorize Holy Scriptures, had kept guard over my heart and my mind that night. Over the years, it would come back to me in times when I need encouragement, inspiration, and protection. I often think of believers who do not or cannot own Bibles and how much they cherish the Word that is within the pages of that Holy Book and within their own minds. How much do we take for granted the multiple Bibles that grace our homes? Will there ever be a time when owning a Bible is a privilege that is taken away from us? I pray not! For now, I work to memorize Scripture and hide it within my heart. It is an honor and a privilege that I do not ever take lightly!

Author: Anita Stafford

REFLECTION QUESTIONS

When did you receive your first Bible?

What is your favorite translation of the Bible?

Have you ever memorized scripture?

What is your favorite verse that you have memorized?

The Future is His Story

For I know the plans I have for you, declares
the Lord, plans to prosper you and not to harm
you, plans to give you hope and a future.

Jeremiah 29:11 (NIV)

I was three years old the first time I stared at the moon endlessly. It gave me a queer sort of feeling in my stomach, like the way you feel when leaning back in a swing. I knew one day, I was meant to walk there, and look backwards in space and time. It felt certain and unquestionable. I knew this, at three. At three, and every year afterwards, I knew, beyond a shadow of a doubt, that my feet were not meant for walking on dust, but floating in zero gravity.

I protected this dream and only told the closest of family and friends who I knew would not question my devotion, assuming it to be the airy thoughts of a listless child. I wasn't insulted when they laughed at my well-laid plans; I was hurt that they didn't understand my heart.

Every step I made was intentional and purposeful. Every class chosen to pave the way to college. Every action guarded to ensure I would not become anything less than a star pupil. I won a free trip, for myself and a friend, from the Discovery Channel, to Kennedy Space Center and Space Camp. For 10 days, I was followed around by squirrels on sticks and a small legion paparazzi. I felt like the real deal! It was really happening! I was as certain that I would become an astronaut as I was that oxygen was necessary for survival.

The summer before my senior year, I received a letter in the mail from West Point, informing me that I was accepted. My Dad (an Army Veteran) was beyond proud. For days, I walked around with the letter in my pocket. I couldn't wait for life to begin. It was all I could think about.

Just before my senior year began, I went with my family and boyfriend of 2.5 years on a trip to a nearby city. Driving in the car with my Jimi, I felt the weight of gravity tenfold when he uttered the words, "I have to deploy. I leave in three months." And in that moment, for the first time in 15 years, I was no longer sure of my future. It felt as if the earth stopped spinning.

The details blend like watercolor on a canvas when I look back. There wasn't really a line drawn in the sand, but I knew that God had made a drastic course correction that would lead me far away from my childhood dreams. I knew, in that moment, that I was supposed to throw myself into loving and supporting this young man who would become my future husband. I expected a barrage of admonishments from my father, but instead was embraced with grace and support. That to me was evidence that God was moving, and that His hand was in the present and the future. I was simply being asked to trust Him.

When God reveals His hand, you better believe it's the winner. There is no amount of good fortune, earthly favor, or well-laid plans, that can compare to the agenda of the Lord.

Just before he deployed that winter, we were married by a Justice of the Peace. It was not an ideal way to celebrate, but we were left with little choice and little time. And now, 17 years later, we are preparing to celebrate our Anniversary and the first birthday of our fifth child. I am walking out my tenth year of homeschooling, and life could not possibly look more different than I had worked so hard to design. The stargazing toddler, now in her mid-thirties, is beginning to see the dreams unfold in her now 14-year-old daughter, who watches every SpaceX/NASA launch, and hopes of becoming the first woman to leave our Solar System.

It may not be in your plans, but when you give it all to the Master Potter, and allow His skilled hands to fashion your future, it'll be nothing short of blessed. The future is His Story, and His plans for us are always better than those we make for ourselves.

Author: Kristin Cash

REFLECTION QUESTIONS

How has the story of your life turned out to be entirely different than you had imagined?

Do you often find yourself wishing you had chosen your own way instead of His?

How can you begin to thank Him for His Story and fully live within the anointed life happening all around you?

Man's Voice, God's Words

If anyone speaks, he should do it as one
speaking the very words of God.

1 Peter 4:11a (NIV)

"You are unshakeably loved and indescribably beautiful." These were the words spoken to me by a co-worker who was responsible for staff care. He was married and very much in love with his wife. The two of them had been walking with me on my spiritual journey as God healed broken pieces in my heart. Sometimes they were both there for a conversation, sometimes only one. At this particular time, it was only the husband. As he spoke those words to me, I knew instinctively that they were not his words. God had a message for me, words He wanted spoken aloud to me, and this man was the messenger.

The next morning as I was spending time with God, He brought the verse from 1 Peter 4 to mind and impressed upon me that I needed to share that verse with my co-worker. I had an opportunity to do that as we worked on a project later that day. I shared the verse and told him that I knew the words he had spoken to me weren't his words, but God's. I had known it instinctively at the time and then God had shown me from Scripture the truth of what I had known. My co-worker heaved a huge sigh of relief. He told me that he had gone home and immediately told his wife what he had said to me. He knew they were God's words, but he was concerned that I might take them the wrong way. She reassured him, saying she thought it was okay. He was being obedient to what God had given him to say. I remember thinking at the time that it was so like God to give my co-worker a message for me and then to give me a message for my co-worker to alleviate his fears at being obedient to share those tender words with me—his single, female co-worker.

God knew that I needed to hear those words at that time in my life. The verse in 1 Peter 4 told me as well as my co-worker that the message hadn't been his. But it also reiterated the truth that the words were God's. That is a powerful truth that God was using to tell me that these words were important. God wanted me to hear the message that He was saying to me that day. He knew the lies that I listened to every day, all day. I recorded them in my journal as I recorded my prayers to Him that day.

I wrote, "The voice in my head is telling me the lies. The voice that whispers, 'You know you are not beautiful. You are fat and ugly and undesirable. No man is ever going to want you.'" Those are the lies You want me to surrender. Those are the lies I have clung to for so long. And the truth You want to put in their place is, 'You are unshakeably loved and indescribably beautiful.' If I disbelieve these words, then I am not trusting You. I know that You are telling me that I need to surrender the lies to You and to surrender to the truth. I want to do this, Lord. I realize I may have to do it again and again. Please, teach me how to live in this truth – that I am beautiful regardless of what I see in the mirror, regardless of what size I wear, that I must believe You that I am beautiful before I'll ever believe anyone else that might say it to me, that I must believe You even if no one else ever says it to me."

Unfortunately, this continues to be an ongoing journey for me. I believe the truth that I am unshakeably loved. I have not, however, arrived at the place where I can believe the truth that I am indescribably beautiful. I wish I did. I continue to hear the other voice, sometimes whispering, sometimes screaming, that I am not beautiful. I continue to look at myself through the same lens that the world looks at me. God wants me to see myself the way He sees me, and I want to be obedient. I want to surrender to His truth. I want to believe His words.

I also want that for you. I want you to know that these words that were spoken to me are also for you. You are unshakeably loved and indescribably beautiful. Those are God's words, spoken by a willing but fearful man to his hurting co-worker. They are also God's words, spoken by this still broken woman to you. Will you hear them and join me on this journey of surrender, of wanting to believe the truth of these words of our Lord? We are unshakeably loved and indescribably beautiful!!

Author: Barb Loewen

REFLECTION QUESTIONS

What are the lies that whisper (or scream) in your head?

What are the truths that God wants you to hear instead? What is the prayer you need to pray in order to reject the lies and surrender to the truth?

Partnering with Holy Spirit

And I will ask the Father, and he will send you another advocate
to help you and be with you forever—the spirit of truth."

John 14:16-17a (NIV)

...That the God of our Lord Jesus Christ, ...may give you a Spirit
of wisdom and revelation, so that you may know him better.

Ephesians 1:17 (NIV)

Who knows that God is always wanting to get our attention? It's not that he's an egomaniac, but that he loves to spend time with his kids. And for me this past week, he has definitely got me looking to him. Five days ago, I injured my back. Who knew that bending down to pick up my chicken's eggs would land me flat on my back and unable to do much at all. For a 'doer' like me who finds it hard to sit still at the best of times it has definitely been a challenge.

I love how God uses all things for our good. I know He didn't cause my back injury, that was all me! Going too hard at the gym and not allowing enough recovery time has its consequences, as I am now finding out. Ever been there? Our enthusiasm about something overriding wisdom in the process? You think I would have learned by now!

Not to mention I have the ultimate personal trainer with me 24/7. Holy Spirit. And yet I still failed to listen to his quiet whisper. 'Be careful, you are going to hurt yourself. ...You're not 25 anymore, you need to rest.' And me arguing back 'I'll be fine... '

That's the thing though isn't it? Holy Spirit doesn't intrude when we won't listen. He just sits back and waits patiently.

We have access to Holy Spirit in every area of our lives. He is with us forever and he speaks truth and wisdom. So why don't we value him as much as we should?

(And when I say we, I really mean me, but I'm secretly hoping I'm not alone.)

We know he's there, We are taught he's with us always. And yet, here I am halfway through my life and I'm still learning the hard way. Is it because we can't actually see him so he's easier to disregard? Or maybe we just take him for granted?

In saying that, I'm a lot further along the journey than I was 10 years ago. But obviously I still have a way to go! Praise the Lord. Learning to partner with Holy Spirit has been a key for me as I mature in Christ as I learn to be led by peace and wisdom rather than self.

So how do we partner with Holy Spirit?

We RECOGNIZE that he is a person, not an ethereal or mystical part of the Godhead (Corinthians 12-11, John 16:7, John 16:13). We REALIZE that he acts as a person and is God. So by nature he is personal (John 16:7, Romans 15:30). We RELATE to him and he instructs us as we include him in everything we do (Acts 13:2, John 16:13).

We REFER to him. Always asking good questions as we go about our daily lives. E.g. Holy Spirit what are you doing? How can I partner with you in this? We REVERE him as part of the Godhead. Nicene creed: '... And we believe in the Holy Spirit, the Lord, the giver of life, He proceeds from the Father and the Son, and with the Father and the Son is worshiped and glorified.'

Just like our Father in Heaven and our best friend Jesus, Holy Spirit is here for us right now. In the everyday, and in the night seasons. And even when we are laid up on the couch for a week. He never leaves us or forsakes us, even in our foolishness, and for that I am eternally grateful.

Author: Kim Beaumont

REFLECTION QUESTIONS

How do you relate to Holy Spirit?

What is one good question you can ask him?

Ugly Hands

For the body does not consist of one member but of many. If the foot should say, 'Because I am not a hand, I do not belong to the body,' that would not make it any less a part of the body... But as it is, God arranged the members in the body, each one of them, as He chose. If all were a single member, where would the body be? As it is, there are many parts, yet one body.

1 Corinthians 12:14,18-20 (ESV)

I have ugly hands. I'm not looking for sympathy, and I'm not saying this out of a false sense of humility. I'm just being honest; if you were to see my hands you'd agree, they aren't pretty! Not feminine, soft, or well-manicured. I have "ranch wife hands." I have my mother's hands. Hands that are weathered, wrinkly, and calloused; nails that are short, chipped, and torn. Hands covered with scrapes, cuts, and dry spots. These hands have rocked babies, fed my family, and doctored wounds on both my children, and livestock. Hands that have stacked and fed bales of hay, saddled horses, halter broke show cattle, chopped ice, and vaccinated calves. I have hands that have served me well; but they are ugly hands.

There have been many times when I've envied the hands of other women; long, slender fingers, manicured nails, and smooth, flawless skin. I've compared and thought my own hands to be embarrassing, so I'd hide them from view, tucked out of sight in my pocket. But then I remember that I have the hands of my mother, and I loved her hands. Her hands were precious to me, I didn't care one iota what they looked like, I didn't compare them to the hands of other women. I knew I loved my mother's hands, and I miss the feel of them on my face or held in my own weathered palms.

Isn't it funny how we compare our lives with those around us, yet seldom realize that others are doing the very same thing? Do we recognize that God doesn't compare at all? I think about all the gifts, talents, and callings I see God refining and using in the lives of other women, and I'm jealous, embarrassed, wanting to tuck my own offerings in a pocket somewhere, hoping He won't notice how unattractive and worn out they are. At times, I've felt my own contribution has been weak and ineffective in the Kingdom building work He has called us to. When all He requires is a willingness, an opening of my hand to allow Him to use it in whatever way He sees fit.

I'm reminded in His Word that we are all part of one great Body of Believers. We don't do this Kingdom Building business alone; it takes all of us, working in tandem together to advance His Kingdom. He uses every one of us, attractive and refined, or broken and weary to accomplish His purposes. He desires to use those less than attractive members just as much if not more to do His work here on earth. He brings us alongside one another and builds us up together. There is no individuality in the Body of Christ, uniqueness yes, but not individuality. We need one another to pursue God's Will...His Will in our own lives, within the Church, and in the world.

Some of the parts of the body are glamorous and attention grabbing, some parts are plain and unassuming. Some members are ragged and worn. The Church is made up of many different parts, the Bible talks about them being the "hands, feet, eyes, and ears" of the whole "Church Body." Christ is the head, and we make up the other parts. Made up of diverse parts; each one is not only acceptable to Him, but also essential to the entire Body.

The Church won't function properly without all the pieces and parts working together in the building of His Kingdom. Pastors, teachers, speakers, writers, worship leaders, children's ministry leaders...encouragement proclaimers, hospitality givers, truth speakers, discernment seekers. It takes each of us, with our individual gifts and talents, working in unison for the common goal of sharing His gospel and encouraging the Body of Believers. If we spend too much time comparing ourselves and what we have to offer God with what other people are offering, we will be ineffective and stagnant in the Body of Believers.

So, I hold out my hands to God, ugly as they are. Hands covered in freckles, wrinkles, and scars, and I humbly submit, seeking how He would use my gifts. I work alongside His people to accomplish His plans and purposes; I don't allow insecurity or comparison keep me from being effective and influential in God's Kingdom Building Work. I focus on the work He has for these hands to accomplish, and I walk forward in boldness when the way becomes challenging. I do all of this alongside the other hands...as well as the feet, eyes, and ears of Christ's Body. Ugly hands, or not, they are beautiful in His sight when used to His glory.

Author: Jana Fraley

REFLECTION QUESTIONS

What are your own gifts and callings that God wants you to use in building His Kingdom?

When you think about your personal part in the Body of Christ, do you feel embarrassed by them or envious about the gifts that others have?

Do you believe your faith is an individual endeavor, meant to be private, or do you believe that we are meant to be part of the corporate Body of Believers?

The Hidden Fear

PART ONE

From the end of the earth I call to you when my heart is faint.
Lead me to the rock that is higher than I...

Psalm 61:2 (ESV)

For you did not receive the spirit of slavery to fall
back into fear, but you have received the Spirit of
adoption as sons, by whom we cry, 'Abba! Father!'

Romans 8:15 (ESV)

The thief comes only to steal and kill and destroy. I
came that they may have life and have it abundantly.

John 10:10 (ESV)

Since I was graduating from university in three months and getting married even sooner, it was time for me to find a job. How could it be that I was finishing up my four years of university training without a clue as to what I might want to do? And even more unclear to me, was why every time I thought about finding a career job with regular hours and benefits and a *boss,* I felt sheer panic, alarm bells ringing, the drawbridge in my brain closing. I warily looked in the want ads in my college town newspaper and saw an ad for an activities person at a local old age home. A part of me knew that would be right up my alley. I could bring my guitar, sing to the patients, start a choir, and plan events, games and crafts. But, at these suggestions, a creepy black blanket of doubt wrapped itself around me and sucked all the life and excitement out of me. It was the voice of doom, an enemy I would come to know as "dread", the dread of failure and exposure. My mind allowed me to focus on a brighter and more acceptable fantasy—I would have a baby and then I would have a reason to stay home and be safe. All of this internal fricassee occurred without my agreement or even knowledge. It would be years before I could begin to sort out the crazy pieces to this mystery puzzle.

I was seven years old when my world crashed down around me. My father who was my warm hugger, piano teacher and avid fan, the foil to my mother's anxious and hand wringing parenting style, died suddenly of a heart attack. He left behind a wife who had not worked in years and who suffered from grave insecurities in her ability to function in a work setting. My only remaining parent was now required to leave "the nest" and go back to work, this time to support herself and three small children. She had an undergraduate degree in sociology and decided to go back to school to become a teacher. If I were to describe in one word what I saw and felt overcame my mother in those years, it would be the word "panic." Panic in the library, panic at the dining room table with books piled up, panic in her bed at night, the light never turned off. It was the wind of panic, it was the storm of panic, flying around our little apartment. Nothing of panic was ever spoken, but all of it flew into my being and wrapped its talons around my ambition, waiting for that day when it would become my guide. Well, that day had arrived.

My unsuspecting fiancé and I enjoyed talking about what marital bliss would be like. We together decided that if we REALLY trusted God, we would not use birth control and leave the timing of babies up to Him. On hearing this, a friend commented that people who trust God for birth control are called parents. And ten months after we were married, we did become parents. After our daughter was born, I immediately felt amazingly relieved. Nursing and caring for her brought me such joy and peace. I never thought to wonder about this, but I do think about it now. What had happened to me that made me so desperate to escape from the world?

Stealthy enemies sneak into our beings when we are not looking, not aware. They come to steal, kill, and destroy all the good hopes and dreams that God originally planted in us. I don't remember ever even getting to the point of dreaming. I was enveloped in the need for protection. I would give up everything for it. The message to my brain was "be safe". All of my inner wranglings were totally hidden from my husband-to-be, hidden from me, and hidden from everyone else. Except God. God always knows the prisons in which we reside and the particular chains that shackle us. He also knows the path to freedom for us and makes that knowledge available to us as we ask Him for it. The path to freedom, however, is not an easy one. It involves our will and daily decisions. I would rather just get zapped into freedom but God wants us to employ our brains, emotions, and will. And we must come to a place of despising our prison cells before we are ready to leave the comfort of them, the supposed safety of them. This requires patience with ourselves and trust in God's willingness and ability to guide us through these very rocky places in our lives.

Author: Miriam Kook

REFLECTION QUESTIONS

How has fear negatively affected your life?

What has helped you combat it?

The Hidden Fear

PART TWO

But Moses said to the LORD, 'Oh, my Lord, I am not eloquent, either in the past or since you have spoken to your servant, but I am slow of speech and of tongue.' Then the LORD said to him, 'Who has made man's mouth? Who makes him mute, or deaf, or seeing, or blind? Is it not I, the LORD? Now therefore go, and I will be with your mouth and teach you what you shall speak.' But he said, 'Oh, my Lord, please send someone else.'

Exodus 4:10-13 (ESV)

There is no fear in love, but perfect love casts out all fear.

1 John 4:18 (ESV)

It comforts me greatly that Moses struggled with self-doubt and fear of exposure. He started out as an overconfident and zealous young man, thinking he could deliver his people by killing an Egyptian oppressor. He was wrong and soon saw himself barely escaping to Midian to avoid Pharoah's wrath. Then he spent forty years in Midian on the back side of the wilderness, shepherding the flock of his father-in-law. When God called his name out of a burning bush, Moses was 80 years old and hardly in any condition to go back to Egypt to deliver a group of oppressed Hebrews. He had gotten soft and probably assumed he would live out his days in obscurity. God had different ideas and we should never assume God is through with us. But we can assume He might call us to undertake activities we don't feel all that equipped to carry out. We might want to say, like Moses, "O my Lord, please send someone else."

Because of the fear I was raised with, I can't tell you how many times I have said that to God. I know that He has promised to never leave me or forsake me. In my head I know that His grace is sufficient for me because His power is perfected in my weakness. But the practical outworking of stepping away from fear has been a slow and sometimes painful and scary process.

I have a story to tell that might illustrate the kind of practical wisdom God gave me when I was facing this giant of fear at a specific time in my life. I tell you this to encourage you that no matter what stronghold you are facing in your own life, God is able to reach in and with enough time and your cooperation and desperation, to give you practical help to enable you to walk out of your own prison. We were living in Egypt and I was working in the music department at the American School. My fears can be very specifically linked to music- music which is both one of my greatest passions and also one of my greatest phobias. I am sure that sounds odd, but we are each such unique creatures with unique problems, aren't we? I had taken a job as a band assistant which entailed handling administrative support for the band teacher. I was in a little room between the band room on the right and the choir room on the left. Every day, I would sit in my little room, typing into a spreadsheet, and listening to the most beautiful music being sung and played by the students in the adjoining rooms. And I would cry. And I would berate myself. In one ear, I would hear, "You're such a loser, look at you. You have a music degree and you love music so why are you sitting here doing this tedious, uninspiring work?" In the other ear I would hear, "Oh no, he's going to ask you to sub for him! You are too afraid to do that, it's going to be too hard. You need to quit this job and be safe!" I had experienced these oppressive voices before but for some reason, at this moment, I recognized them as the enemy of my soul who was attempting to discourage me and fill my heart with despair. And suddenly, God was there, giving me practical wisdom on how to escape from this prison of fear. The voices had been my constant companions since childhood but it was time to put them out. How?

In my specific situation, I was faced with addressing them and telling them they were not welcome anymore. Showing them the door and saying, "I reject you and your words of condemnation and fear, and I reject your plan to make me hopeless and frustrated and afraid- now get out!" Then I was to turn my body in the opposite direction and address God, saying, "I welcome you and your words of truth, words that affirm me and tell me you love me, words that build me up and show me the way to use the gifts you have given me." I was to speak to God about promises in the Word that He had made to me and to welcome those promises to do their work in me. I began to put this plan into action. Every time those voices of fear tried to surreptitiously hijack my emotions, I would do what I knew I needed to do. It took a little while, but soon the accusing, negative voices started to recede and I began to feel free from the constant presence of fear.

For me, this is how God's perfect love very practically, and with my co-operation, cast fear out of me. I still have to remind myself to this day to not let any of those negative, hateful, discouraging words take up residence inside of me. And to always, and very deliberately, welcome God's Word into my heart.

Author: Miriam Kook

REFLECTION QUESTIONS

Have you discerned any stronghold, a habitual pattern of thought, that has taken up residence in your heart or mind?

Do you believe God can help you walk out of your specific prison?

How can you and God work on this together?

Remembering with Gratitude

Seek the LORD and his strength; seek his presence
continually! Remember the wonderous works that he has
done, his miracles and the judgements he uttered.

1 Chronicles 16:11-12 (ESV)

I opened my gratitude journal this morning and it landed on a page already covered in gifts. The words caught my attention, and I began to read the familiar words in my handwriting. Memories began to flood my mind of the moments captured. I had given thanks and even felt grateful enough to pin down these thoughts in my journal; yet, here I was again, reliving the gratitude for all the ways the Lord had blessed me.

I felt a bit nostalgic and missed some of those precious seasons I was reading about, but it evoked such gratefulness for having been given the moment in the first place.

Remembering is important to the Lord, the One who never needs His memory jogged. He calls His people *to remember,* many times throughout Scripture. Most often He calls us to remember the Lord our God, remember Him. Why might that be?

It seems rather easy to remember the Lord when hard things happen, when trials roll in and we desire a way out. It seems easy to remember the Lord when prayer requests fill my journal, and my heart is desperate for a miracle in my life or in the life of someone I love. But how quick am I to remember the Lord when I finally get the answer I have been praying for? How often and for how long do I remember the Lord when that long-time prayer request gets answered and I have what I wanted?

David felt the pleasure of God as the Ark of the Covenant came to land in the Temple of God. People offered thanks offerings and peace offerings for this accomplishment the Lord had brought about through them. But that was not enough for David, the man after God's own heart. No, David insisted on remembering the Lord with intentional gratitude.

"On that day, David first appointed that thanksgiving be sung to the LORD by Asaph and his brothers, 'Oh give thanks to the LORD, call upon His name; make known His deeds among the peoples!'" (1 Chronicles 16:7-8) And he goes on in verse twelve to call to the remembrance of the people who their God is and all He has accomplished. "Remember the wonderous works He has done."

David was a man who took note of God's gifts and recalled them often, reminding his own heart of the goodness and character of God. He was intentional to give thanks for who God is and what He had done. I wonder if he even kept a gratitude journal and some days allowed time to reminisce over all the blessings of God in and through his own life.

Author: Mariel Davenport

REFLECTION QUESTIONS

Do you have a gratitude journal? If so, take a moment to flip back and thank God again as you remember His goodness to you. If not, how about starting one today?

Begin by writing down three gifts from God's hand and thank Him for His goodness.

The Hydrangea

But he said to me, 'My grace is sufficient for you, for
my power is made perfect in weakness.' Therefore, I
will boast all the more gladly about my weaknesses,
so that Christ's power may rest on me.

2 Corinthians 12:9 (NIV)

My daughter was born one week before my birthday and Mother's Day weekend. As a gift to myself, I bought a beautiful white hydrangea, my favorite flower, to celebrate Mother's Day and the birth of my beautiful new baby, my third child, and the only girl. I brought home my new hydrangea and set it on the back deck with plans to plant it in the garden the following weekend.

And there it sat, all summer. And then all winter. And then for two more years after that.

Shortly after my daughter was born, she began to have several health struggles that took us many months to figure out. At the same time, my eldest son, then six, was beginning to struggle with developmental and behavioral issues, and my middle son with insomnia and anxiety. My own health was also starting to decline.

By the time my daughter was three, we had been to two family counselors, two parenting seminars, and read twelve books, only to feel like we were no farther ahead with our boys. By then, though my daughter's health concerns had finally resolved, mine had gotten worse. I was in constant pain, severely fatigued, and battling severe anxiety, and brain fog.

The dead hydrangea sitting on the back deck served as a daily reminder of all the ways I was failing as a wife, a mother, and a woman. The life I dreamed

I would have when I bought it, my newborn daughter cradled in my arms, rapidly slipping through my fingers like dry sand.

Our family was in trouble. *I* was in trouble.

It became clear that we would need to make some extreme changes in order to survive. So, in a terrifying step of faith, we decided to sell our home, and move to a smaller, one level house in a less expensive neighborhood.

The day we decided to move, I finally took the hydrangea off the deck and planted it in the backyard. I was sure it was dead. How could it not be? But the yard needed some work before we could list the house, and what was the harm in just throwing it into the ground to see what would happen? Worst case scenario, I would replace it later.

I knelt in that little backyard garden, tears streaming down my cheeks, and with all the faith I could muster, I put the shreds of my heart in Jesus' hands and planted that stupid, dead hydrangea. *Here you go Lord,* I thought, *Let's see if You can do anything with this.*

And much to my shock and delight, within two weeks, there were tiny green leaves sprouting from the branches, and four weeks after that, beautiful white blooms bursting in every direction!

This small miracle, this little resurrection there in my tiny, ordinary, nothing-special backyard, was a profound message clearly impressed on my weary, worn-out heart. *Just because something looks dead, doesn't mean it is.*

Once again, I knelt there in my garden, tears streaming, only this time with gratitude. The promise of His faithfulness birthed new hope in my heart that it would be okay. And it was. It would be a whole year before we were able to find a new home that met our needs within our budget, and it was a very stressful time, but God is good, and faithful, and the work He *begins,* He completes.

It wasn't until several years later that I learned that hydrangeas symbolize gratitude, grace, and beauty. It was a delightful little realization, but to me, that is what they had symbolized all along. When we finally did move to our new home, one of the first things I did was plant another hydrangea, and every time I see those gorgeous, giant blooms, I feel the deep love of the One who makes all things grow, and can bring growth in all things. And it was only just the beginning.

Author: Jennifer Hayes

REFLECTION QUESTIONS

Is there a situation in your life that "looks dead?" What caused you to lose hope in that area?

Release this "dead" situation to the Lord's hands. Ask Him to breathe new life into it.

Write this situation and your prayer down in a journal. In faith, leave the page next to it blank, so you can write down His answer when it comes.

The High Cost of Peace

Blessed are the peacemakers, for they
shall be called sons of God.

Matthew 5:9 (TLV)

Those that serve to keep us safe and protect the peace, both at home and abroad, pay a high price for our safety and freedom. My husband, after 37 years in law enforcement was disabled from the only career that he ever had, due to multiple injuries and the degeneration of his health. Yet that was the call that God had placed on his life, one that he gladly followed, regardless of personal cost. Our first responders and service men and women, in most cases, chose that career out of a desire to help others. How costly that choice has been for generations of them and for their families. Jesus said that the peacemakers would be blessed and called "sons of God." What does that mean for the ones we love who keep the peace?

In 1 John 3:1 (TLV), the writer states "See how glorious a love the Father has given us, that we should be called God's children—and so we are! The reason the world does not know us is that it did not know Him." In Romans 8:16-17 (TLV), Paul writes that "The Ruach Himself bears witness with our spirit that we are children of God. And if children, also heirs—heirs of God and joint-heirs with Messiah—if indeed we suffer with Him so that we may also be glorified with Him."

Simply said, the sons (and daughters) of God are joint heirs with Christ, and as such will share in His inheritance. We understand that each person must come to accept a personal relationship with Christ to be saved, but I believe that Christ is offering a special recognition here to those who serve to establish, protect, and keep the peace for all of us. As a woman who may be a wife, mother, or daughter of a peacekeeper who bears the scars both externally and internally from their battles, what can you do to help them? What do we as women do best? Nurture, love, listen, and hug, in the good times and the bad times, even when we do not understand the struggles that may be going on inside of them. We may need to learn to let go of our desire to jump in to fix or solve challenges, as that often furthers the hurt by making our loved one feel "less than" what society expects a warrior or peacekeeper to be, strong and immune to danger or injury. Rely on the Ruach, the Holy Spirit, to guide you. Keep your own spiritual practice up, and tap into the Power Source, Jesus Himself, to show you just what to do to bless the peacekeepers that belong to you and me.

Author: Anita Stafford

REFLECTION QUESTIONS

Do you have a Peacekeeper in your family?

If so, what can you do today to thank them for their service and show love and/or appreciation?

If you do not have a peacekeeper in your family, is there something that you can do to show your appreciation for those who serve?

Take some time today to read through the Beatitudes in Matthew 5:3-12. Do you see yourself in any of the verses? If so, where, and why?

Presence or Performance

Jesus answered them, 'This is the work of God, that
you believe in Him whom He has sent.' So they said
to Him, 'Then what sign do you do, that we may see
and believe you? What work do you perform?'

John 6:29-30 (ESV)

Prayer requests are not hard to come by these days. I sit down in the morning before the Lord and He easily brings to mind the friend who is grieving, the loved one who is sick, the elderly, the trials, and pains in my own life. It is a growing list every day it seems.

That doesn't even count the bad news we saw last night on TV that needs prayer; politics, growing cases of the virus, economic issues. It can feel so overwhelming and I feel so small as I bring it all to the Father in the morning.

As I sat before Him again this morning, the thought occurred to me afresh that He was really listening. He was present in the room with me. I sat soaking in the truth of that moment. He is near to us and makes His dwelling with His people, it is His way.

I began to pull out the list of prayer requests. I know He wants me to bring Him all that concerns me, that the trials and details, He desires to hear my heart even though He knows it already. He is after relationship. Relationship means casting my cares into His lap.

This morning in my Bible reading in John 6, I sensed this question surface from the Lord, "Are you after My presence or my performance?"

Ouch.

I do so love His Presence, and I love the sense of Him with me throughout my day. But how often do I bring a "to-do" list to God and expect performance over simply desiring Presence?

When my boys were small, they loved to cuddle. They would crawl into my lap silently after naptime, complete with their favorite blanket and stuffed Elmo. It was the sweetest. I would inhale their scent and enjoy their warm, fresh-from-sleep velvety soft skin. They didn't say anything, nor did I. It was just a moment of presence. Time together. I enjoyed that they just wanted to be with me. No expectations. No Christmas list given. Just a moment to sit with Mama.

There is certainly time for requests, and He desires that. But what if our heart and motive started with a desire for His Presence? Crawling into the Father's lap during the hard trials to spend time with Him, acknowledging He is near without asking Him to perform on our behalf. That is real intimacy and relationship. In those precious moments with my boys, bonds were built between us, not when I bought their requested item at Target, but when I cuddled them, sang over them, and we enjoyed one another's nearness.

Author: Mariel Davenport

REFLECTION QUESTIONS

When was the last time you just sat in His Presence? Enjoy the moment knowing your Father is near to you and loves you and delights in you.

Can you relate to moments like this with your own children or nieces and nephews? How differently might you see God's response to you when you consider that He feels this way about you?

My Cry for Freedom

PART ONE

In my anguish I cried out to the Lord, and
he answered by setting me free.

Psalm 118:5 (NIV)

God often gives me pictures when He is teaching me something. Not always, but often I have a mental image that comes with a spiritual lesson. That's what happened when I finally got to a place of emotional anguish and I cried out to the Lord.

In my mind's eye, I pictured myself lying facedown in the throne room of God, crying out for freedom. All I could pray over and over were the simple words, "I want to be free." I was there, weeping as I drove to work in the early morning hours, praying, "I want to be free." I was there as I worked, trying to hold back the tears so that my coworkers wouldn't see my desperation, praying, "I want to be free." For days, that scene played repeatedly in my mind. Facedown before God's throne, pleading, "Lord, I want to be free. Please, set me free." I don't remember how long that desperate prayer lasted. And I'm not sure just when God answered that prayer. But I do know that one day I realized I was finally free.

We all have chains. Sometimes they are from things that happen to us, things that are beyond our control. But often, those chains are there because we put them there. We pick them up and wrap them around ourselves. We might not recognize them as chains, or maybe they don't start out as chains. But that is what they become.

I found this verse from Psalm 118 along with a few others that spoke of freedom at a point in my spiritual journey when I knew that was what I wanted. I wanted to be free. I wrote them out on note cards and hung them on the walls of my bedroom. And yet, somehow, I wasn't quite ready. God knew I needed to recognize the chains first. He also knew that there was an idol behind the chains and that I wouldn't see the chains if I didn't see the idol. And just like the chains may not start out as chains, so an idol may not start out as an idol.

I graduated in the early 80's when women were advocating for their rights and we were supposed to want a career. I didn't. I wanted to be married and to serve in ministry with my husband. There was nothing wrong with wanting that. It wasn't an idol at that point. But as the years went by and that amazing man didn't come along to fulfill that desire, I went through a gambit of emotions. And the questions came. What is wrong with me? Why doesn't anyone want me? Why did God create me with this strong desire to be married and then not answer my prayer for a husband? Doesn't He love me? Isn't He good? And somewhere along the line, this desire turned from something that I wanted to something that I believed I deserved. And it became an idol. And with the idol came the chains. And over the years those chains wrapped tighter and tighter.

My journey to freedom took a long time. I wish it hadn't. I wish that I had begged for freedom a lot sooner than I did. But I can't go back and change things. All I can do now is live in the freedom that God has given me. And I am loving living in freedom. I'm not saying that life is perfect. It certainly isn't. But I am no longer bound by the chains that my desire for marriage and a husband created. I am living this life of singleness that God has given me, and I don't feel like I am missing out. I know that He is good, that He gives good gifts, and He has given me a good life. And I am thankful that when I cried out in anguish to Him, He answered by setting me free!

Author: Barb Loewen

REFLECTION QUESTIONS

What desire do you have that God hasn't yet fulfilled?

How can you know if this desire has become an idol in your life?

What could life look like if you were free from the chains an idol creates?

My Cry for Freedom

PART TWO

O Lord, truly I am your servant; ...you
have freed me from my chains.

Psalm 116:16 (NIV)

There have been times when I wished that it hadn't taken me so many years to find freedom. But then I remember those days of desperation – tears as I drove to work, fighting back the tears at work, picturing myself facedown on the floor before God's throne begging for freedom, only able to pray the few words, "I want to be free." One day as my memory took me back to that scene, I realized that as I lay there on the throne room floor, I experienced God as my King. I was a lowly petitioner, and yet I didn't feel anything from God but welcome. I was welcome there in His throne room. Even though I was laying facedown, begging, there was no shame, no re-crimination. I was welcome there for as long as I felt the need to stay. I don't remember how long that was. But I recognize the sense of welcome when I recall those days.

And I remember the sudden realization – a long time later – that God had answered my prayer, that I was free from the chains that had bound me for so long. I remember the lightness that freedom had brought me, that I still experience.

I wouldn't give up that time on God's throne room floor for anything. Even as I wrote about it again in my journal, I was there in His presence, seeing myself as I lay prone before Him. I encountered that feeling of welcome, recognizing in the memory what I hadn't in the original experience. As I once again entered that memory, I realized the welcome, but there was more God wanted me to see. Beyond feeling welcome, I also felt His love. Even as I laid there before God, broken and pleading, His love was surrounding me, filling the throne room.

If I look at this image from a human perspective, love from the King is not what I would expect. I was coming to Him asking for freedom from an idol that I had chosen, which I had put before Him in my life. I wanted freedom from the chains that I had helped wrap around myself. He should have had less compassion for me. He should have said, "You got yourself into this mess; you get yourself out of it." He could have looked at my choice to put something else before Him in spite of all He has done for me, and He could have chosen to turn away from me. But He didn't. Instead, He welcomed me with overwhelming love. Because of His mercy, He didn't give me what I deserved. Because of His grace, He gave me what I didn't deserve. I had gone against His word and desired an idol more than I desired Him. And because of His love, when I returned to Him asking for help, He willingly reached down and freed me from the chains, releasing me from the hold this idol had in my heart. And I haven't stopped thanking Him for His grace and mercy and love.

We as humans are so easily distracted by things in this world. It happened to Adam and Eve in the garden and has continued to happen to all of us down through the ages. We see something that we want, and we pursue it. Very often there is nothing wrong with those desires. If I want to purchase a new outfit that I like, it can be an innocent desire and there is nothing wrong with fulfilling it. But other times, an innocent desire can turn into something more. Initially, my desire to be married was innocent. There is nothing wrong with wanting to be married. But when I continued to wait on God to fulfill that desire and He continued to say no, my desire changed from something innocent to an idol. This can happen with any desire and we need to be careful to guard our hearts, to protect ourselves from letting our desires become "over-desires." That is a term I heard in several Tim Keller sermons to which I have listened. We allow our desire to become too important and it comes between us and God. It becomes an idol. And with the idol, comes the chains. When that happens, only God can free us, if we but ask.

Author: Barb Loewen

REFLECTION QUESTIONS

What desire in your life has the potential to be an idol?

What can you do to prevent that from happening?

If you think something has already become an idol, what are you willing to do to release it and ask for freedom?

Erasing the Line Between the Sacred & the Secular

Here's another way to put it. You're here to be a light, bringing out the God colors in the world. God is not a secret to be kept. We're going public with this, as public as a city on a hill.I f I make you light bearers, you dont thinkIm going to hide you under a basket, do you? I'm putting you on a light stand. Now I have put you there. Shine! Keep an open house;be generous with your lives. By opening up to others, you'll prompt people to open up with God, this generous father in Heaven.

Matthew 5:15 (MSG)

G rowing up I dreamed of becoming a nun. I'm not Catholic. Ha. But it was the only way I could see as a girl that I could serve God. Fast forward to my late 20s, when I started to attend a solid bible believing church. I was quite relieved and very excited to discover that there were numerous ways to serve without becoming a nun. Relieved because by that time I was married with two babies. Excited because now I could discover what it was God wanted me to do!

And so the journey began. I served in kids church, the kitchen, young adults, women's ministry, connect groups, worship team, preaching team and the list goes on. If there was a hole, I would fill it. The joys of being part of a small church. Can you relate?

It was both a delight and a challenge. But in my mind I was 'in ministry' and serving both God and my community and I loved it.

And yet there was still something not quite right. I couldn't put my finger on it. We were taught and encouraged that to serve God looked like signing up and being there. Serving and loving our brothers and sisters in Christ.

And then I began to notice something. The church was full of families and people from all walks and seasons of life. Hard-working people who loved God and loved the local community. But not all of them were able to commit to the privilege of serving in the church. After work commitments, family priorities and much-needed rest from a long work week they didn't have anything left to give. Understandably so. And what they did during the week, didn't seem to be valued as much as working within the church. There was an unspoken pressure. Well, if I'm really honest it wasn't just unspoken. To be a really committed Christian, you would serve in the church. Working outside the church was seen as a second class ministry. As much as we were taught that we were all equal in God's eyes. All sons and daughters of the King. Working and serving in the church was the priority and dare I say, almost revered. And for a young woman who equated her self worth and identity in 'doing' I thrived. Until I didn't.

I watched my husband and many people like him love God with everything they had, work long hours for a family they adored and come home from church feeling unappreciated and undervalued. All because they didn't work or serve in the church. Have you ever experienced this? Or is it just me?

"You are an instrument God chooses to move through" (Isaiah 8:1).

Nowhere in this verse does it say that 'God chooses to move through instruments in the *church only*'. The church is not a building. We are not contained by four walls. We are all instruments that God moves through, no matter where we are. In our homes, workplaces, at the gym, in school and at church.

God is erasing the line between the sacred and the secular. And I am so excited! He did not put the line in, it was never meant to be there. Jesus worked and did life beside lawyers, tax collectors, fisherman and ex prostitutes. The 'them and us' divide, that line between the sacred/ church and the secular/ the marketplace really began back with Pharisees and the Sadducees. A religious spirit that has invaded Christianity and in many ways divided many of God's people. And now it is being erased for good!

The Ministry of serving God is a 24/7 assignment and privilege. Whether it is at the local church, or at the grocery store in the checkout line. Maybe it's in your local business or down at the community garden. Could it be, dare I say it even at the local bar?

We have the responsibility as God's representatives to reach out and shine Jesus no matter where we are. We are not to insulate from the world. We are to invade the world. Be the light where there is darkness. Show people the answer where there are questions. Exhibit the love of Christ, where there is confusion and fear. And we can't do that if all of our lives revolve only around home and church.

I will say it again! God is erasing the line between the sacred and the secular. He values all of our work, as we dedicate it to him and include him in our lives 7 days a week. I want to encourage you today. You are the light that the world needs to see. Don't hide it under a basket or just within the walls of the church. The world needs to see Jesus in you! Your job, your time spent with littles or teens or grand babies is not second class ministry. You are valued, you are loved. You are seen by him! And the world is a better place with you in it!

Author: Kim Beaumont

REFLECTION QUESTIONS

What is your ministry in this season?

How can you be Jesus to those around you?

Spilled Milk

If any of you lacks wisdom, let him ask of God, who gives to all liberally and without reproach, and it will be given to him.

James 1:5 (NKJV)

As a parent, I've often used the phrase, "No use crying over spilled milk" over the years when facing a mess made by one of my two children. They haven't always been spilled milk messes, but were messy, nonetheless. Many times, it was what I would say to myself as I've wanted to sit and cry over messes that have interrupted and disturbed my days.

I do have a story about spilled milk; however, it isn't what you're probably thinking. I wish it were a story about one of my kids spilling milk while I patiently bent down to their level, saying "don't worry sweetie, no use crying over spilled milk." However, it wasn't my child that spilled milk...it was me...and it was on purpose.

When my daughter, Hannah, was about 3 years old, I was the coordinator of our local Moms group. As a young mom of a preschooler, I really struggled with being on time. One morning was particularly hard as I tried to get myself and my slowpoke of a daughter ready and out the door by 8 am to make our bi-weekly group meeting. When I say that she was a slowpoke, I'm not exaggerating. She was the child that, when asked to hurry, she would somehow hear, "Go slower!" My patience had reached its limit that day; she had finally finished her bowl of cereal, only to ask for more. I poured her just enough to soak up what milk was left in the bowl, thinking that would satisfy her; it didn't. Her immediate whining let me know she wanted more milk in the cereal. Since she still had milk left in her glass, I just poured it into her cereal bowl and walked away feeling proud of my resourcefulness and time management strategy. But her whining became a full-on temper tantrum, complete with screaming, tears and banging on the table, insisting that I needed to get "fwesh milk from the fwidge." My nerves were shot, and my stress level hit the roof.

This is where I wish I could say I handled my daughter with wisdom, grace, and patience, but I did not. Instead, in a moment of utter frustration, I took the bowl of cereal and milk and I dumped it right in her lap! Even now, 20 years later and knowing my daughter was not traumatized by this event, I am still filled with shame. What kind of a mother does that? I do have to say the shock factor worked to some extent, because her tantrum ended and she just looked up at me with big blue eyes saying, "This a mess Mama!" She wasn't kidding; I had a mess of milk and cereal all over her, the chair, and the floor. What exactly did I accomplish? Now we were running even later, and I had no wisdom, no grace, and no patience!

A dear friend and Christian mentor shared this verse from James with me around that time. I especially love the translation from The Living Bible, "If you want to know what God wants you to do, ask him, and he will gladly tell you, for he is always ready to give a bountiful supply of wisdom to all who ask him; he will not resent it" (James 1:5, TLB). One thing I have consistently prayed for throughout my years as a mother is wisdom. And yet, wisdom is often illusive.

What I've found to be true is that God often gives wisdom at the times of our worst failures and ugliest messes. There is a certain kind of wisdom we only find in the midst of messy trials and difficult situations. Wisdom that helps us see how we can prevent those trials in the first place, or wisdom in understanding the reason why God allows some trials to come into our lives. The Bible doesn't say to seek wisdom from google or Social Media, it doesn't say to look for it in self-help books, political leaders or the newest worldly philosophy. It says to ask GOD, and He will give it without judgement, hesitation, or condition.

Too often, as parents, we believe God isn't concerned with our "spilled milk moments"; those little disruptions and struggles in our daily lives. However, what I've discovered is God is not only concerned with them but wants us to lean in close to Him for wisdom in ALL situations; those moments when we fail, hurt, struggle and question where to go next. He doesn't give wisdom partially or some of the time, He gives it liberally and whenever we ask. Seek wisdom from God, for everything from spilled milk to difficult decisions and hard trials. He gives it without fail or reproach.

Author: Jana Fraley

REFLECTION QUESTIONS

Have you ever had a "spilled milk moment"? A time when you were in the middle of a big mess of your own making?

How has God brought increased wisdom into your life through some of your worst messes?

What is the difference between Godly wisdom and worldly wisdom?

Saved from a Futile Life

Knowing that you were ransomed from the futile ways
inherited from your forefathers, not with perishable
things such as silver or gold, but with the precious blood
of Christ, like that of a lamb without blemish or spot.

1 Peter 1:18-19 (ESV)

Have you ever been struck by the futility of life? Futility means emptiness, fruitlessness, hollowness, senselessness. Just reading those words can put a damper on your whole day! Being raised in a nonbelieving home, I saw firsthand what it meant to live by futile ways leading to a futile outcome. Since in our family God did not exist, we were cast solely upon what people thought. My single-parent family was not highly esteemed, the apartment building we lived in was rundown and made me feel like I was a second-class citizen. When I struggled with friend problems, or school problems, or sister problems, or boyfriend problems, I was on my own to figure out my way through them. My solutions, as can be imagined, were not well thought-out and they often led to outcomes that were worse than the original problem.

But what made life feel so futile was that my dad had died suddenly of a heart attack when I was only seven and there was no explanation of why that could happen, no hope that I would ever see him again, and no perceived purpose to the suffering his death brought into my life. No one in my life held out any hope. Everything I was taught to be important: education, getting a good job, being a good person, marrying and having a family, all seemed futile if someone important to you could just up and die. I didn't buy into these goals that were preached to me, but I wasn't sure how to find a better way to think.

I remember the first time as a new believer, I read these words in 1 Peter: "Knowing that you were ransomed from the futile ways inherited from your forefathers, not with perishable things such as silver or gold" (1 Peter 1:18, ESV). I was struck by how God was aware of this awful, futile feeling I had been raised with. I realized that a heavy price had to be paid and was paid for me to escape from the deadening feeling of emptiness that every human being in the world lives with. The Bible is so insightful in addressing the futility we humans feel and it states what Jesus, the spotless Lamb, did for us, shedding His precious blood to provide the necessary ransom for our redemption, lifts us out of the futile lives handed to us by our parents. 1 Peter goes on to say in verse 21, that "Through Him you have confidence in God who raised Him from the dead and gave Him glory so that your faith and hope are in God." Jesus' resurrection absolutely puts to death the notion of our lives being futile. We who believe put our confidence in God who sprung Jesus from death and the grave and gave Him glory! And He has promised that when Jesus was sprung from death and the grave, that we were sprung with Him! This life is not the last word! Jesus' death and resurrection says so!

Author: Miriam Kook

REFLECTION QUESTIONS

What situation have you been in that has made you feel that life is futile?

How could the death and resurrection of Christ help you combat that futile feeling?

After This

After this I looked, and behold, a door standing open in heaven!

Revelation 4:1a (ESV)

After I put on the white gown and said, "I do," I became a wife, changing everything about my status, name, and life. After I birthed a child, I became a mother, changing my identity and heart in ways I never would have imagined.

There are moments in life that bring with them an "after this" that marks us forever. Sometimes the "after this" moment comes with a welcomed change, but sometimes it does not. After we said our goodbyes to my Dad for the last time, he went Home to Jesus. The loss marked my soul deeply.

The current climate of this culture and world is certainly a season that *after this* will likely have lasting change on every person who was alive through 2020. Global pandemic, illness, deaths, racial issues, hatred, even the politics in the United States are scarring our land, our neighborhoods, and our own souls. After this, we will be changed, but will it be for the better?

I used to think that after going through something life-changing that we would automatically learn the lesson, be changed, grow from it. I'm not convinced that is the case anymore. We may come through a difficult season marked, but we may come forth bitter, hard, and cold, or we may come forth compassionate, gentler, and closer to Jesus. Until we are intentional to use that season to press into the Lord and allow the Holy Spirit to adjust our perspective, bear fruit to His glory and know Him better, then we risk coming forth from a trial with the root of bitterness that Hebrews warns against (Hebrews 12:15). According to Hebrews, we need to see the grace of God in our circumstance to keep from the bitterness.

Growth and maturing through a trial take purpose and intention. It takes watchfulness to notice His hand of grace in and through it. It takes leaning into the Lord so we might better guard our hearts. The Lord desires to refine us through trials, making us more like Himself. He desires to bring us forth as gold.

After this, the world will see face masks differently, handwashing and cleanliness will be looked at with a more critical eye. Certainly, we will see race and political divisions from a new perspective and speaking our minds will likely have become more about power and being heard than principles and listening.

After these things we will be different and our souls will be scarred, but how will you and I come forth? Will we cooperate with Jesus and let Him complete His good work in us through it making us more Christ-like? Will we let Christ shine through us to a hurting and lost world, taking every opportunity to glorify Him and point others towards Him?

Like the wedding day or the birth of a baby, will we allow the status of our world to shift and just shift with it? Or will you and I find purpose and intention and press into Christ through this so that after this we will be more effective salt and light in this world?

Author: Mariel Davenport

REFLECTION QUESTIONS

What is your season of "after this" in your own life that has marked you?

How can you press into the Lord, even right now through stillness and prayer to allow Him to do His good work in your own heart through this?

The Pain of Perfection

God shows his love for us in that while we
were still sinners, Christ died for us.

Romans 5:8 (ESV)

I still remember the day I had to force my son to learn to ride a bike. Yes, you read that right... *I had to force him!* Did I mention he was four and the bike had training wheels? He was having trouble coordinating his feet to push the peddles one at a time. He was frustrated with himself immediately, threw his bike on the ground, crossed his arms, and screamed at me, "THAT'S IT! I'M NEVER GOING TO RIDE THIS BIKE! I HATE IT!" And then he kicked it.

But I was convinced that I knew better. I mean, *what kid doesn't like riding a bike, for heaven's sake?!* So, for the next 45 minutes, I forced him. I made him stay on the bike, while I bent over him, my hands on his little knees pushing them down one at a time to make the pedals turn, while he screamed at me the whole time. Neighbors came out onto their porches to see who was torturing this poor child.

Finally, after nearly an hour, his body learned the rhythm, and he was peddling on his own. After that, he wanted to ride his bike everywhere. "I LOVE my bike, Mommy!" Well, I hate to say, "I told you so," but... I knew he would love bike riding. I knew the fun and freedom would be worth the effort of learning. He just had to get past the pain of being a beginner.

I realized that day that my little four-year-old boy had a perfectionist streak a mile wide, and unfortunately, he got it from me.

It took me until the age of 39 to learn to play the piano, because I wasn't Mozart the first time I sat down at the keys. It took me 10 years to finally start a blog, because it involves a learning curve in both the tech part as well as the actual writing. As I've gotten older and more self-reflective, I've realized that this has been a pattern in my life. There are many things in my life that I've never experienced because I knew I wouldn't be "perfect" at it right out of the gate. I hated the pain of being a beginner.

Eight years later, I now have three children, two of whom are perfectionists. Not the trait I would have chosen to pass on. The irony is not lost on me that in order to help my children to overcome the lie of perfectionism, I would first have to overcome it myself.

A blog I've followed for years has this tagline:

It doesn't have to be perfect to be beautiful.

I've been thinking about this tagline a lot lately. I think I'm realizing, slowly, that beauty is actually found within the *imperfections*. More to the point, in *our imperfections*. Where else is God's glory more evident than when it pours through the cracks of a broken vessel?

The story of my life could have many endings to this tagline:

It doesn't have to be perfect to be meaningful.

It doesn't have to be perfect to be valuable.

I don't have to be perfect to be loveable.

That last one is a real kicker. A few years ago, a wise friend said:

"Preach the gospel to yourself every single morning. When the most important question of your existence has already been answered, everything else is just details."

And so, I do. I'm preaching these things to my own heart. Regularly. Daily, even, because:

God shows his love for us in that while we were still sinners, Christ died for us (Romans 5:8).

The truth is that perfection is a mirage. It doesn't actually exist. It's a unicorn. Something we see in pictures on the internet, in magazines, in movies, in stories, but never in real life. This mirage of perfection contains within it many lies, and they open a void in the soul that this world cannot fill. I am still learning to name these lies, to pull them out by the root and plant the truth down deep in its place. It's messy, painful work, but critically important if I want to let my children be who they really are, and still help them become who God wants them to become. *They're just waiting for me to go first.*

Overcoming perfectionism will likely be a life-long work for me. However far I've come, there's always farther to go. Yet if my Father, who is perfect, does not require perfection of me, how can I require it of myself (or anyone else, for that matter)? But He delights in a child who is teachable, a child on the cusp of learning. He delights in the beginner. That's why His mercies are new every morning (Lamentations 3:22-23), not so that I can get it perfect this time, but so that I can be a beginner, and begin again tomorrow.

Author: Jennifer Hayes

REFLECTION QUESTIONS

Is there a lie of perfectionism that you have believed? What is it?

What does "beginning again" look like for you?

Sunday Lunch

Now people were bringing little children to *Yeshua* so He
might touch them, but the disciples rebuked those who
brought them. But when *Yeshua* saw this, He got angry. He
told them, 'Let the little children come to Me! Do not hinder
them, for the kingdom of God belongs to such as these. Amen,
I tell you, whoever does not receive the kingdom of God like
a little child will never enter it!' And He took them in His
arms and began blessing them, laying His hands on them.

Mark 10:13-16 (TLV)

Peer pressure is a powerful thing, and I wondered if that was the driving force behind the question that my two daughters brought to me one day. "Mom", they said, "why don't we ever get to go out to lunch after church on Sunday like everyone else does? We really want to eat out! Please Mom!" I tried to explain about budget and needing to be careful about where we spent our money, but all they could comprehend was that they wanted to go out to eat, everyone else got to and why couldn't we?

I was a single parent working three jobs at that time. Yes, you read that right, three jobs! I worked full time in the mortgage industry as a loan processor, I worked part-time on the weekends at a Christian bookstore and I babysat two little girls, who went to the same school as my girls, overnight two nights per week for another single mom who had to travel with her job. When we were a two-parent household, we had put our girls into a private Christian school at our church, and we had rented an older, but comfortable home, close to both work and church. When my husband left us and moved out of state, I was desperate to keep the girls in the same home and school. My reasoning was that this was the fourth home and fourth school in three years for them. My husband had moved out, moved back, and now was gone again. My mind was reeling from all the changes and I was set on avoiding more changes, if possible, for them.

So, this question, this desire to go out to eat, left my mind twirling like the juggler at the circus spinning plates. We did not get to do very many "fun" things these days, although they thought getting to go to work with me at the bookstore was great fun. They had access to innumerable books and videos, got to talk to customers and "help" mom at work. I thanked God every time I went to work there that the management let me bring the girls with me so that I did not have to pay for any additional childcare. We certainly did not get to go out to eat very often at all, and I shudder today to think about how many times we ate ramen noodles and peanut butter and jelly sandwiches because they were cheap.

My two girls had such a simple, child-like faith, that they had demonstrated to me over and over. They were well-behaved, loving to me and more importantly, they loved God. As I prayed about this desire of their young, innocent hearts, a confidence rose in me that God would provide a way for this. So, we sat down, the three of us, and talked about it. I explained that if we were careful about where we spent our money the rest of the week, we would go out to lunch after church, starting this very next Sunday. They wanted to go to Burger King and that is where we wound up. To this day, it is etched in all three of our minds. I had a Whopper Junior meal, and they both had a chicken finger meal. Drinks, fries, the whole works. The grand total was $10.64. It may not sound like much and today I am not sure there are many places where one person could eat for that now. But we all ate to our satisfaction and then off they ran to play on the indoor playground, giving me some time to breathe and reflect. Week after week, this was our routine. Church, Burger King, $10.64 and play. I never missed the money because God provided it week after week. I was able to keep the girls in their school until we eventually moved to a new job, new home, and new marriage. But that is a story for another day!

Through their child-like faith, I learned that all our desires, big and small are important to God, when are hearts are in the right place. What started out as a plea by two children to go out to eat after church on Sunday, became a story that we tell time and time again about how God cares for us, wants to give us good gifts and He provided for our needs and desires, even the ones that only cost $10.64 and involve fast food. Their simple faith became a landmark for me in my memory of how much God loves all His children, then, now, and forevermore.

Author: Anita Stafford

REFLECTION QUESTIONS

When have you seen God provide a simple request for you?

Have you ever seen God meet a prayer of your children?

How can you have a more "child-like" faith today?

Beloved. You are Priceless.

Anyone who belongs to Christ is a new person.
The past is forgotten, and everything is new.

2 Corinthians 5:7 (CEV)

G rowing up as a military child, I grew to appreciate small windows of consistency and adventure. Moving often gave me the ability to start fresh, meet new friends, forget the past, and press on towards achieving something new. I didn't realize I struggled with friendships until I was a middle school student, riding a band bus on our way to a statewide competition, only hours after receiving one of the worst haircuts I have ever had to date. It was reminiscent of Reba McEntire, which should have been flattering in the best of ways, but on my awkward, preteen demeanor, it felt more like a mistake than an intentional style.

I remember sitting in the stylist chair, a salon owned by a sweet family friend. I was slowly and methodically gazing through each page of the latest hair style magazines, with elegant photos of celebrities daunting their sought-after dos, and I chose this style specifically to be acknowledged and respected. My stylist, skilled with years of experience, did a beautiful job, recreating it perfectly. The problem was not the haircut. It was my lack of self-confidence and lack of self-worth.

I was often the third wheel. To be quite frank, I can hardly recall a time that I was not. On more than one occasion, I was leered away from things and places, so my friends could make a quick escape. During one incident, a parent had to return for me at a mall in a town that was 350 miles south of my home. I was terrified, in a day before cell phones, and I literally had no idea if they would ever return for me.

I carried this lack of self-confidence and self-worth into my teen years, allowing decisions to be forced upon me for fear of losing relationships. This led to years of self-harm and neglect as an early adult when I often found solace in one too many glasses of wine. The sexual abuse, mingled with my own sense of guilt and shame, and I felt like an imposter in my own skin.

The early years of my marriage were littered with misunderstanding, and far too often, I found myself crying in isolation, hoping my tears would be the catalyst for my husband to draw me closer. That never happened. It is an unhealthy way to live, responding to the desperate cries for attention in your spouse. Healing and prayer are the only saving graces in this type of situation.

If we do not allow the Lord into the broken places of our soul, we will continue to walk wounded. Believing in Christ, and accepting Him as our Lord and Savior, is not enough, it is just the beginning. Christ desires to have a deep and meaningful relationship with us, not a dominion over us.

We must be willing to invite Him into every corner of our soul; to shake off all the rugs and wipe down every finger smudged counter. When we invite the Holy Spirit into our one broken heart, the old is gone and the new has come. A genuine relationship with Him means we desire to sweep it all out so that we can begin to live fresh, full lives, as He intended for us to before all the pain, mistakes, and heartache. Day by day, as we draw nearer to Him through prayer, worship, and soaking up His Word, we will begin to become aware of our priceless worth, because of His indwelling in us, not because we are accepted, seen, or acknowledged.

There will come days when we fall back into old habits and forget who we are, but these are brief and momentary struggles. God is our ever-constant source of help in times of trouble, and we are made in His image. This means that we have the ability to live to our full potential, without the limitations our experiences have taught us. We are free from self-condemnation, worldly judgments, and past trauma. These things do not define our worth. Our worth is found in the unfathomable grace of Christ.

Author: Kristin Cash

REFLECTION QUESTIONS

How has Christ reminded you of your priceless worth in Him?

Do you feel that the old is gone and the new has come? How?

In what ways would you like to see Him set you free from past experiences?

Seek His Face

Look to the Lord and his strength; seek his face always.

Psalm 105:4 (NIV)

I follow Emily P. Freeman on Instagram. One day on her Instagram feed, she asked the question, "When you picture God, what image comes to mind?" What a great question! I asked it of a few friends and colleagues, and it led to some interesting conversations. One friend and I both said that when we pictured God, we didn't picture a face. We found that curious. Around the same time, I came across this verse in Psalm 105 where we are instructed to seek God's face. That meant that even though I might not see a face when I picture God, I am instructed to seek it. So, I looked up the word "face" in my Bible's concordance and began to read the many verses that were listed.

Several of the verses speak about God's face shining upon us, or the light of His face shining upon us (Psalms 4:6, 31:16, 67:1, 80:3, 119:135). Most of these verses are requesting that God would make or let His face shine upon us. As I thought about that, I thought about how a person's face lights up when someone they love walks into the room. It is an unconscious act which shows their pleasure at seeing the one they love. It shows their delight. But these verses in Psalms appear different than that response. They are a request for God's blessing or salvation. They are an echo of the blessing the priests were to say over the Israelites (Numbers 6:22-27).

What does it mean to seek God's face? That was one question that came out of my search. I looked at the story of Moses where we are told "The Lord would speak to Moses face-to-face, as a man speaks with his friend" (Exodus 33:11). But later in the same chapter, when Moses asks to see God's glory, he is told that he cannot see God's face and live (Exodus 33:20). This seems like a contradiction, but I see it as there is more here that I need to understand. What is God saying? I wonder if what God was intending for us to know is the type of relationship He had with Moses. Is the crucial phrase in that verse, "as a man speaks with his friend," and "face-to-face" is simply describing that relationship in a way that we could understand, rather than referring to an actual face-to-face encounter? And when we are instructed to seek God's face, are we being told to get to know God, to build a relationship with Him? That is what I would do with a person if I wanted us to become friends. Why wouldn't I do the same with God? I would spend time with them, ask questions, share stories of my life, open up about myself to them. I want to do that with God. When I spend time in His word, when I ask questions and seek out answers in Scripture, when I write in my prayer journal, these are all things I can do to get to know Him. I believe that is how I can seek His face.

I thought again about the way someone's face lights up when they see a loved one. I wondered, does God's face ever light up when He looks at me? I believe God's Word says it does.

"The Lord your God is with you, he is mighty to save. He will take great delight in you, he will quiet you with his love, he will rejoice over you with singing" (Zephaniah 3:17).

It's hard for me to imagine that God delights in me. I want to, but it's easier to imagine God scowling at me. We often see God that way, as a God of displeasure. But if I seek His face, if I want to know Him better, then I need to see the truth in verses like Zephaniah 3:17. I need to see His eyes turn to look at me, see the love that fills those eyes, see the smile that breaks out on His face, watch His face light up in delight. And then I need to listen as His voice breaks out in song as He rejoices over me. Can you imagine that? Do you long to imagine that? I sure do!

"My heart says of you, 'Seek his face!' Your face, Lord, I will seek" (Psalm 27:8).

Author: Barb Loewen

REFLECTION QUESTIONS

What's your answer to Emily's question, "When you picture God, what image comes to mind?"

What does it mean to you to seek God's face?

Do you have a hard time imagining God delights in you? If so, why do you think that is?

The Pursuit

Draw near to God and He will draw near to you.

James 4:8 (NKJV)

My story of choosing Jesus isn't a grand miraculous testimony. I didn't have an angel meet me, or fall off my donkey and hear a voice. It didn't even seem all that life-altering in the moment. But of course, it was.

I grew up hearing the Bible as bedtime stories. Mixed with fairy tales and adventures with *The Secret Seven* and *The Hardy Boys*.

I knew about baby Jesus in the stable at Christmas and His terrible death on the cross at Easter. I was taught the Lord's Prayer and the children's song, "Jesus Loves Me." We faithfully attended church every Christmas and Easter.

And yet, there was this pull. This yearning for connection with Him deep inside of me that has never left me.

Psalm 139:5-7 (NLT)

You go before me and follow me.
You place your hand of blessing on my head.
Such knowledge is too wonderful for me, too great for me to understand!
I can never escape from your Spirit!
I can never get away from your presence!

I know now it was the Holy Spirit guiding me and leading me. But back then all I knew was that I wanted more! And I wasn't even sure what 'more' looked like.

When I was 12, I decided I wanted to be a nun. Even back then I could feel Him calling me. That indescribable need to be closer to God and to live for Him. Why a nun? you may ask. Truth be told, it was the only option I was aware of where women could serve God. Plus, Audrey Hepburn looked beautiful when she played a nun. And Sally Field in the old television show, *The Flying Nun* looked kind of fun too! Who wouldn't like to teach about God and fly whenever the wind took up!

That internal pull continued throughout high school, leading me to a couple of youth groups; where my mum promptly pulled me out after hearing they wanted to baptize me. Coming from her Catholic background, she thought they were a cult.

God continued to draw me. There were empty churches, where I would sneak into and just 'soak up the atmosphere.' Even back then I could recognize the presence of God drawing me closer. I just didn't have words to explain it. Oftentimes I would be sitting by myself in those churches. No one there but me and Him and great acoustics. I would sing the only 'God songs' I knew. "Jesus Loves Me" and "Amazing Grace." Tears would flow down my cheeks, my heart ready to explode. I knew God could hear the song of my heart and it overwhelmed me.

It still astounds me how much God loves us no matter where we are. My story written here sounds so precious and beautiful, and it is. But there was a whole other side of my life filled with hurt, abandonment, rejection, and brokenness. A life complicated with divorce, confusion, late night parties, and abuse. And yet, He still loved me! He continued to pursue me, even in all the mess, and He never gave up on me.

Sometimes we believe the lie that we need to have it all together. We need to be worthy of God's love. But that is a lie from the pit of hell! His love is so wide, so deep, so extraordinary that it reaches us, no matter how deep the mess is that we are in. His love reaches out and pulls us up. It never gives up. He is always there waiting for us to reach out to Him. God is not afraid of the mess or the darkness of life. In fact, that is where He shines best. Where there is light no darkness can stand!

Author: Kim Beaumont

REFLECTION QUESTIONS

Can you remember a time or a moment where you could feel his pull?

Is there a mess in your life, God is wanting to pull you out of?

Learning Contentment

Not that I am speaking of being in need, for I have
learned in whatever situation I am to be content... I
can do all things through him strengthens me.

Philippians 4:11,13 (ESV)

Perhaps the greatest lesson on strength I've learned was taught by my mother-in-law, Barb. She displayed strength in every form: mental, emotional, spiritual and even physical. I often say that my mother-in-law was the strongest frail woman I knew! Diabetic from the age of 8, Barb dealt with health problems almost all her life, but never allowed that to define her or slow her down. She was a force to be reckoned with! Standing 5'5" and barely weighing 125 pounds, Barb's strength was not something you noticed when you first met her. Whoever came up with the saying, "she's little but mighty", must have known my precious mother-in-law!

I fell in love with Barb long before I ever entertained the idea of actually dating her son. She was the director of the local library, and I, with an insatiable hunger for books, was a frequent visitor. Her smile lit up a room and her laughter was contagious. We enjoyed many conversations about the books and authors I loved, and she always made sure to set aside anything she thought I'd enjoy. When I began dating Mike, it was hard to choose who I enjoyed spending my time with the most, him or his mother! In those days of dating and early marriage, I felt blessed by my mother-in-law. She was easy to love, and she loved me like a daughter, unconditionally and completely.

God was preparing my heart for the day our roles would change. A few years later I'd become more than just her daughter-in-law, but also her caregiver. God created a strong bond and deep love between the two of us, which carried me through several difficult years of caring for Barb's physical needs as her health declined. Together, my mother-in-law and I learned the hard lesson of "contentment in whatever situation".

I spent each day with Mike's mom caring for her basic needs. I also had a busy toddler to deal with at the time. I was exhausted and stretched thin. Many days I fought the feeling that, although I loved Barb, I didn't like her much. She could be stubborn, demanding, and irritable and I was self-involved and selfish. Those days were trying, but now I see they were years of refinement and faith strengthening. I had to ask God each day for the ability to love my mother-in-law beyond what I was feeling. I think she had to do the same for me. We were often prickly and impatient with one another, and resentment began to grow.

Contentment was not something either one of us could claim, and misery was a constant companion. I'll never forget a particularly hard day when we both were fighting tears, anger and bitterness. I couldn't do anything right, and I became increasingly short-tempered with Barb. I

looked at her, ready to react with a sharp word on the tip of my tongue, when God gave me a vision of Barb as when I first met her. I remembered her as she used to be: physically able to walk on her own and take care of herself and her family, her immediate smile and joy at seeing every person who walked through the doors of the library, her easy laughter, how she would lovingly hold my daughter on her lap and read to her, or when she shared sweet memories of my husband when he was a little boy. God gave me eyes to see her like He saw her, as His beloved and precious daughter who was dealing with devastating health issues and disappointments.

I quit fighting the tears and started crying; but instead of tears of frustration and hurt, I was overwhelmed with love and gratitude. I took her hands in mine and asked if we could pray together. What followed was one of the most amazing and precious gifts I've ever had. In praying for one another I experienced a love for Barb that went beyond what I was feeling; it was a love based on how God saw and loved my mother-in-law, not on our current circumstances.

I'm not going to say that every day after that was easy and without conflict; but I will say that the days I gave to God, He blessed us both with contentment and joy in each other's company. A few years later I had to say goodbye to my precious mother-in-law. I miss her terribly and am so thankful for that time we had together, and for the strength God gave both of us to endure a less than ideal situation. Through Him and Him alone we were able to truly find contentment and strength for the trials we faced as we relied on the strength that He gave to us.

Author: Jana Fraley

REFLECTION QUESTIONS

What situations in life have brought you discontentment?

How did you handle those situations?

Looking back, can you see how God worked through situations that threatened to make you discontent?

The Lizard & Me

PART ONE

The lizard you can take in your hands, yet it is in kings' palaces.

Proverbs 30:28 (ESV)

Humble yourselves, therefore, under the mighty hand
of God so that at the proper time he may exalt you.

1 Peter 5:6 (ESV)

I don't know why, but I have always wanted to be famous. When I was a little girl, I thought if I could just get some talent scout to stand outside my window and listen to me singing in my bed, that he would come up to my second-floor apartment in Queens, NY and give me a Hollywood contract to sign right on the spot. I remember sitting next to the window in my room at night and singing songs like, "I Feel Pretty" and "You'll Never Walk Alone" in my most beautiful 8-year-old voice. No one ever showed up.

Fast forward 10 years and I had become a believer in Jesus. Somehow, those thoughts of becoming famous did not leave me. I just "baptized" them into the faith. I figured I was a Jewish girl who believed in Jesus, I wrote songs, I had deep thoughts about the Bible, and I wasn't bad looking. Plus, I was probably going to marry this awesome Jewish believing guy who also had deep thoughts about the Bible and wasn't bad looking. I thought all of these things would make us unique enough to qualify us for Christian stardom!

Unbeknownst to me, fame was not exactly what God had in mind. In fact, it wasn't even close. Life and parenthood came upon us, and we were quite overwhelmed. Every thought of fame blew away like a flimsy hat on a windy day. But, as with most things, the desire for attention and accolades didn't die. Left unchecked, it went underground and turned into frustration every time I saw someone else doing something "for the kingdom." But God doesn't leave us in our miserable states. He gives us what I call keys to our situations, keys to the things that lock us up.

My husband was teaching Old Testament, Hebrew, and Greek at a small Bible college in the middle of nowhere. Our neighbors were cows and because the salaries were so meager, housing was provided for us. Because we were subordinates in a very hierarchical community, we probably had the ugliest, smelliest apartment on the campus. I was miserable and very vocal about it. I didn't deserve this! I appealed to God to help us find a way out of that apartment. My husband tried bringing our complaints to the heads of the school. The staff told him we didn't even deserve a bed in God's estimation and that we should be happy we got one. I didn't know which God they were talking about but it wasn't the one I had signed up with!

Sometimes when we are caught up in negative thoughts, feeling resentful and angry and put upon, God can use the Bible to speak deep truths to us which can set us free from our myopic viewpoints. One day, in the midst of my bad attitudes, I was reading the Bible and this verse jumped out at me. It was Proverbs 30:28, which says, "The lizard you can take in your hands, yet it is in kings' palaces." What did this verse mean? God was essentially saying to me, "Learn how to be small and to be content with smallness. Be a lizard, small and unassuming, so I can take you in MY hands and put you where I want you." That's what Jesus, the God who created the whole universe, did when He became a man. Philippians 2:6-7 tells us that although Jesus was in the form of God, He did not count equality with God something to be grasped, but that He emptied himself, by taking the form of a servant, by being born in the likeness of men. He wasn't thinking about Himself and how to exalt Himself, He was thinking of us and what might make Himself available and knowable to the people He loved. And that's really what I wanted anyway. To be in God's hands and to do whatever He called me to do that would make Him available and knowable to the people He loved. Even if it meant dealing with living in a yucky place! Even if it meant that my dreams of being "famous" would never come true.

Author: Miriam Kook

REFLECTION QUESTIONS

What childish wishes have remained with you into adulthood?

What situations have you found yourself in where you needed God to give you keys to get you through?

The Lizard & Me

PART TWO

Now Jesus loved Martha and her sister and Lazarus.
So, when he heard that Lazarus[a] was ill, he stayed
two days longer in the place where he was.

John 11:5-6 (ESV)

W hile I was struggling with having to live in a really unpleasant place, I happened to be reading the story of Jesus' friend Lazarus, you know the brother of Mary and Martha. In this story, Mary and Martha weren't arguing about who was going to make dinner, they were pressing cold cloths on their brother Lazarus' forehead to try to bring his humongous fever down. Lazarus had been sick for days but his raging fever was not breaking and he was unable to hold any liquids down. The sisters were so scared that they sent a runner off to look for Jesus. "Now Jesus loved Martha and her sister and Lazarus. So, when He heard that Lazarus was ill, *He stayed two days longer in the place where He was.*" I stopped reading. Did I read that correctly? Jesus loved these three, and so He didn't come when they desperately needed Him but stayed where He was for two more days- on purpose? That made no sense and yet I felt that the Holy Spirit was trying to speak to me... about God's kind of Love. God's Love didn't necessarily come when people deemed it important, but waited, which made it look like He didn't care.

Jesus was good friends with these folks and spent lots of time in their home in Bethany overlooking the Golden Gate and the Old City. Jesus was not at their home when Lazarus became ill, but he was down by the temple mount area getting in trouble again with the religious leaders. Mary and

Martha had seen Him heal fevers like this before and so they were hopeful that He would come quickly to lay hands on their brother, His friend. The runner finally returned but he didn't think Jesus was coming since He had turned away and continued the conversation He had been having after hearing about Lazarus' illness. How strange and out of character that seemed to them, and to me.

Could it be that Jesus knew something that Mary and Martha didn't know and was making decisions based on that knowledge? Yes, He knew that His Father wanted to not merely heal Lazarus, but to raise him from the dead and to teach not just Mary, Martha, and Lazarus but a whole crowd of people and US a far more important lesson about who Jesus was and the extent of His power. He wasn't about to short-circuit what His Father was aiming to accomplish through Lazarus' death and resurrection.

This was another deep lesson for me in understanding that it is not that God doesn't answer prayer. When we cry out to Him to come and save us from our circumstances and He doesn't do what we ask, it isn't that He doesn't care or is too busy for us. He is oh so aware and He absolutely does care. He does love. His love answers to a higher call though, His Father's call. He sees the big picture. He responds with the wisdom from above and we are expecting Him to answer us according to earthly wisdom. We have to trust His timing. We have so much to learn. So, He leaves us in stinky apartments.

A day or two after these revelations, I went to the grocery store with my toddler son. On exiting the store, he bent down and picked something up off the ground. "Aaron put it down!" I chided, but he turned and handed it to me. It was a tiny rubber lizard. I looked at it, looked up and smiled. "Let's go home", I said to Aaron, and we three, Aaron, the lizard, and I walked down the hill to our stinky "king's palace."

Author: Miriam Kook

REFLECTION QUESTIONS

Have you ever struggled with unanswered prayer in your life or the life of someone you care about?

What has God taught you through unanswered prayer?

A Revealing Test

He said this to test him, for He Himself
knew what He would do.

John 6:6 (ESV)

Oftentimes as a mom with young boys, I would find myself asking them, "What would have been a better choice?" after having broken up an argument between them. Their brown eyes staring blankly at me as if considering this question for the first time. Often the firstborn would offer up obvious solutions that he figured I wanted to hear. "Don't hit him." "Let him have the toy." "Ask for the toy rather than take it."

Their solutions fell flat most of the time because the reality was, I knew what the answer I wanted was. I wasn't trying to figure it out by asking them. I wanted *them* to get to the right answer, to get to repentance, forgiveness, and grace one another.

With large crowds following Jesus with grumbling bellies and hearts that desperately needed a Shepherd, He turns to His twelve with a question, "Where are we to buy bread so these people may eat?"

He didn't feel at a loss and need their limited abilities of problem-solving. He was testing their hearts to reveal to them that what *they* needed was Him, the Bread of Life. Would they turn to Him with, "Jesus you are our only hope and solution and You alone are enough," or would they flounder and try to solve their problem with their own limited means? They did what my young boys would do and what I often try to do myself. They physically looked around and tried to fix their own problems apart from the power and strength of Jesus.

We have 220 denarii, or we have this kid's lunch. No, you have Jesus, the Living God who called you to this place and has drawn near to you. You have every spiritual gift in the heavenlies and lack nothing pertaining to life and godliness through the knowledge of Him (Ephesians 1:3, 2 Peter 1:3). Every single one of us in Christ has the same Jesus.

We waste so much time and energy chasing our own tails instead of pausing during the test, trial, or difficulty and seek Him. We do not have to think up our own solutions and muscle through to figure it all out. We have to draw near, know Him in and through the difficulty and rest in Him. Pause. Pray. Ponder the Word. Let Him give you direction and peace as you move forward.

Author: Mariel Davenport

REFLECTION QUESTIONS

What do you need direction or a solution for right now in your life?

Could you pause, pray, and ponder the Word right now, laying your questions at His feet and seeking His peace and direction?

The Potter and the Clay

Yet you, Lord, are our Father. We are the clay, you
are the potter; we are all the work of your hand.

Isaiah 64:8 (NIV)

My first encounter with a real potter's wheel was an eye-opener. Humbling, to say the least. I had always thought pottery looked so easy, so effortless. But there is a hidden artistry in the hands of the potter that cannot be observed, only felt.

As I sat at my own wheel, attempting to copy the actions of my friend, a seasoned artist and potter, I listened to her explain the breathtaking process of this beautiful art.

First, the lump of clay must be slammed down hard onto the wheel to create a tight seal between it and the wheel, and it must be exactly centered. If it is even slightly off center, the vessel will be ruined when it spins. If it does not adhere to the wheel, it will be destroyed.

Second, the vessel must be kept wet. Potters keep a bowl of water and sponge close by, and douse the vessel constantly. If the clay becomes too dry, it will crumble and be destroyed.

As the wheel spins, the potter's arms must be held at a precise angle, hands in a precise position, and fingers in just the right spot. Too much pressure, and the vessel will be destroyed. Too little and it won't take form.

Once complete, the newly formed vessel must be fired in a kiln to change the molecular structure of the clay so that it will not dissolve when submerged in water, otherwise, it will be destroyed. If it is *not* fired, it will become brittle when it dries, crumble and fall apart. Without the fire, the vessel will be destroyed.

It was a far cry from how I always interpreted the experience of what it must mean to be molded by the Potter's hand! I used to read these verses and think being molded and formed by the Potter sounded not unlike a spa experience, a much needed massage for sore muscles. Maybe it's uncomfortable in places, painful even, but oh, you feel so much better afterwards! Secretly, though, I wondered why it seemed so much harder for *me*. Why couldn't I seem to take shape? I had yet to understand that the vessel cannot form itself, nor does the vessel design itself.

What that little lump of clay becomes is in the limitless imagination of the divine Creator. *How* it becomes is in the artistry and intimacy of His masterful hands, purified and solidified by fire.

The apostle Paul wrote: "We are hard pressed on every side, but not crushed; perplexed, but not in despair; persecuted, but not abandoned; struck down, but not destroyed" (1 Corinthians 4:8-9). The plans of the Potter are to prosper us, and not to harm us, plans to give us hope and a future (Jeremiah 29:11).

I finished my little beginner pottery project both frustrated, and in awe. It looked easy, this pottery business, but it was not. I had intended to make a coffee mug, but all I was able to manage was a tiny trinket dish. It was not what I envisioned, but it was all my unskilled, amateur, little hands could produce.

Do you know what happens when God sits down at the potter's wheel to make art? *You do. You happen.* Fearfully and wonderfully handmade by the Master Artist Himself. He who has created you, He who has formed you, He has redeemed you, and called you by name. You are His. When you pass through deep water, when the river rages, you will not be swept away. When you pass through the fire, you will not be consumed, the flames will not set you ablaze. You. Are. His. (Isaiah 43:1-2, paraphrased). The careful and skillful work of His hands is painful, *but hidden within the forming is the redeeming.* For the work He begins, He will finish, and the work of His hands cannot be destroyed!

Author: Jennifer Hayes

REFLECTION QUESTIONS

Is it a relief to know that the vessel cannot form itself? Why or why not?

How is God forming you? Where are you feeling pressed?

Does knowing the process of how pottery is made help you respond differently to the pressures in your life? How?

Running Shoes and Jesus

And I heard a loud voice from heaven saying 'Behold,
the tabernacle of God is with men, and He will dwell
with them and they shall be His people. God Himself
will be with them and He shall be their God.'

Revelation 21:3 (NKJV)

Several years ago, I began running in effort to help lose weight and improve my cardio condition. Not that I particularly like running, but because it is something, I can do with no gym membership, a minimum of equipment, primarily a good pair of running shoes, and a couple sets of workout clothes. I do love the feeling when I am done of knowing I accomplished a good workout. However, that alone was not enough to keep me motivated to keep running, especially in the early morning, so I began signing up for half-marathon races. I am the type of person that once I commit to something, and especially if it has cost me money, I stick with it to the end. Along the way, I discovered that I really enjoyed the accomplishment of the long distance running. Over a period of about five years, I ran a total of 10 half marathons and a 10K. But something told me to push for more. I had already reached my weight loss goal and had now added gym workouts to my regimen, so it was not that I needed more conditioning. But the thought would not leave me alone. So finally, I did it. I committed to run a full marathon in 2019, 26.2 miles.

The training was time consuming. I ran three days per week, which is all that I could accomplish working full time and doing weight training in the gym. Saturdays were my long runs. In the beginning, they started out at about three miles, but over the course of the 6-month training program, they worked up to 20+ miles. Since I only run about 4-5 miles per hour, those long runs are a minimum commitment of five hours by the time you stretch, run, cool down, and stop for water and more stretching.

My Saturdays toward the end of the training were spent running and recovering from running. But at the beginning of 2019, I had also made a commitment to be consistent with my devotionals and time with the Lord at the start of each day. So, my Saturday routine began with a pre-workout drink, a protein bar, my Bible, my devotional, and Jesus. For several days in a row, the study had been on the concept that God is with us, Immanuel (Matthew 1:23). We are filled with the Holy Spirit (Acts 1:5). God Himself dwells in us in the form of the Holy Spirit. Jesus said that He would be with us, even to the end of the age (Matthew 28:20). Day after day, my study reinforced this idea and it began to settle within my spirit as never before.

This Saturday, I felt the presence of the Lord so strongly as I completed my devotional. Pre-workout drink done, protein bar eaten, water bottle filled up, Bible and devotional put away, I continued praying as I sat on the hall tree near my front door and laced up my running shoes. The house was quiet. I was the only one awake that early in the morning. So, I felt no reservation about talking to The Lord out loud. "Well, Jesus," I said. "If you truly are with me wherever I go and in everything that I do, and I know that You are, I sure hope that You like running because that is what we are going to do today." Immediately, I heard the voice of The Lord reply to me. "I love running with you," He said. Tears sprang to my eyes as I realized that what I do, what I love, and where I go is important to God, and not only that, but He truly is with me. He enjoys being with me, even when I am running.

Over the years, Jesus has been my constant companion on my running journeys. One day as I set out, I told Him "Lord, I am really tired today. I am going to need a little bit of help here to finish this run." Less than one quarter mile later, I was beset upon by two small yipping dogs at my heels. This was definitely motivation to pick up my pace. "Really, God, really?" I said. "Two yipping dogs. That's Your idea of help here?" I felt the laughter of the Lord settle over me as I continued my run. If I ever doubted that God has a sense of humor, He has shown it time and time again as we talk and run together. I have found that while running, my mind is at peace. My subconscious has only to focus on the next step and the next breath. That leaves my conscious mind to listen to God and talk with Him. I have had so many divine inspirations during our time together running, from business management ideas to themes for devotionals yet to be written. Our time together running has become so precious to me. He has proven to me that He truly is Immanuel, God with us.

Author: Anita Stafford

REFLECTION QUESTIONS

Have you ever heard the Spirit of The Lord speak to you?

When do you feel that you hear Him most clearly?

What things do you find interfere with spending time with God alone?

A Glimmer of Hope

We have this as a sure and steadfast anchor of the soul, a hope that enters into the inner place behind the curtain, where Jesus has gone as a forerunner on our behalf.

Hebrews 6:19 (ESV)

Hope doesn't need permission from our flesh to activate. It permeates out of the darkness, like a tiny spark awakening a room when a crack of light finds its way in. This is Jesus alive in us. This is the gift given by Christ when He told His disciples that He must leave them so that He could send The Helper. This Helper, residing within us, is the same power that raised Christ from the dead. This Divine Power, activated in our souls the moment we accept Christ as our Savior, doesn't require any ritualistic behavior on our part to display His power. It simply is. Christ, aside from the embodiment of the Holy Spirit, was alone in the tomb He was gently laid to rest in. There was not the physical presence of another living person there to perform a powerless task to activate this power that raised Christ from the dead. The Holy Spirit, residing in us, does not depend on us to raise up a banner of Divine Power. He exists without our permission and in spite of our weakness, He is The Great Helper.

Early February 2015, I was 18 weeks pregnant with what was nothing short of an absolute miracle of a baby. Six years of infertility, not even one glimmer of hope from a monthly cycle existed for an entire six years, and then one day, just before Christmas 2014, I felt "off" and decided to take a pregnancy test to torture and amuse myself. To my complete shock, it was unquestionably positive, yet I persisted to take an additional 10 more tests to convince my jaw to close. Now, 18 weeks pregnant with our first boy, I was teaching a class that my two daughters were attending, when I felt a sudden gush of fluid run down my leg and into my shoe. I was certain my water had broken, and I was terrified. How on earth was this miraculous baby going to survive at 18 weeks?

"No. God. No." My stomach hit the floor with this fluid as I quickly excused myself from the room, trying not to alarm my daughters, and quickly ran to the bathroom. To my horror, it wasn't my water. My jeans were entirely soaked through with blood. I couldn't contain my panic, and within seconds, friends flooded the bathroom to see what was wrong. All I could do was try to take another breath as I desperately prayed for God to fix whatever was wrong. A friend grabbed my phone and keys out of my classroom for me, and promised to sit with my girls. The blood continued to flow, each breath becoming harder than the one before it, as I made my way to the car, and called my OB. They quickly brought me back to a room, and while I was lying on a bed, bleeding without ceasing, I made a quick call to my husband, and begged God to save my baby.

The next few moments were a blur as two friends made their way into my room, and a nurse wheeled in a bedside ultrasound machine. "God. I don't want to see. Please! Please! Save my baby!!" I kept repeating aloud, "So much blood. It's just so much blood. What could be wrong?" as the nurse tried to calm me down and my OB made quick work to get to my bed. Waiting. Waiting. Waiting.

It felt like an eternity. All I knew is I was lying in a bed, covered with blood, and could not recall the last time I felt the baby move. My world felt small and dark, and with each passing second, it got smaller and smaller until it felt as if there was no light in the world at all. I felt entirely alone, even though I was surrounded by people, friends holding my hands. The screen turned on. He placed the wand on my swollen belly, and all I could see was darkness when I looked at the screen. It felt empty and cold. But then, all at once, the light, without prompting, flooded in, and a shard of hope shot out of my breaking heart, splitting the dark, cold room in half, as I heard the most beautiful sound in the world, the sound of my son's heart beating, steadily away. I could not believe what I was hearing. It was nothing short of a miracle. And then, my OB, sounding much relieved, "He is okay. Fluid level looks good. Heart sounds perfect." And, in my absolute shock, while blood continues to pour onto the bed, I ask, "How is this possible? It's so much blood. How is this physically possible? He is completely unaware of the trauma happening here."

After further testing, it was revealed that a large hematoma had burst near his placenta, and although I continued to bleed for several more days, hope needed no prompting. I couldn't have mustered it in my own strength, even if I had tried. This Living Hope sustained me every moment of the day. It was as sure and constant as the bleeding, and yet it was more powerful than the dark that tried to engulf me. Hope is alive.

Author: Kristin Cash

REFLECTION QUESTIONS

How has God sustained you with unprompted hope?

When has God redeemed something you thought was dead?

Have you shared your story in safe circles to encourage others?

The Lord is My Portion

I say to myself, 'The Lord is my portion;
therefore I will wait for him.'

Lamentations 3:24 (NIV)

Because I am part of a mission organization, I occasionally have an opportunity to speak at chapel in a local Bible College. I am always fascinated with the way God gives me something to share when I have those opportunities. It is usually from a lesson that He has been teaching me and one that stands out clearly to me came from this verse in Lamentations. He also gave me a great object lesson to make the point.

I arrived quite early before chapel to get everything set up. I placed a table at the front of the chapel and borrowed six bus bins from the kitchen. I had made two cream pies that I took with me for the lesson. I cut one of them into six pieces but made sure that they were not equal in size at all. One slice was very large, another not much more than a sliver. The others were somewhere in between. I dished up the slices onto six plates and placed the bus bins upside down, one covering each slice of pie. The second pie I left in a large container on the floor beside me so that it couldn't be seen.

I shared with the students about the ministry of the mission with which I serve. Then I shared what God had been teaching me, ending with Lamentations 3:19-24. I told them, "This is a passage I have read many times, but when I read it recently, God showed me something new. And to help illustrate it, I need seven volunteers." I asked six of them to stand behind the table, one person by each of the bus bins. The last student I had stand beside me. Then I asked the six students to lift the bus bins and to hold the plates up so the rest of the students could see what was there. As you can imagine, there was a lot of laughter when people saw the varying sizes of pie slices.

Sometimes in life our "portion" seems big and sometimes it seems small. It's easy to look at others and compare our portion with theirs, especially when theirs looks bigger than ours.

But verse 24 says, "The Lord is my portion."

At this point in my talk, I pulled out the whole pie and handed it to the student who had stood beside me. And I continued by telling them...

As I read that verse last week, the realization I had was, "If the Lord is my portion, then my portion is huge! It's massive! It is actually beyond my comprehension!"

In Psalm 73, which scholars believe was written by Ezra the priest, verse 26 says,

"My flesh and my heart may fail, but God is the strength of my heart and my portion forever."

As a priest, Ezra didn't receive a portion of the land like other Israelites. But he recognized that God was his portion, his inheritance, his provider. When we go through times of suffering and affliction, when we aren't sure how we will make ends meet, when we are tempted to look at our neighbor and compare our life with theirs, we need to remember that the Lord, the God of the Universe and beyond, is our portion. Our portion is not just a piece. It's the whole pie.

Author: Barb Loewen

REFLECTION QUESTIONS

What does "The Lord is my portion" mean to you?

When are you tempted to compare your "portion" with others?

How does thinking of God as your portion change your perspective on your life?

Memorial Stones

He told them, "Go into the middle of the Jordan, in front of
the Ark of the Lord your God. Each of you must pick up one
stone and carry it out on your shoulder—twelve stones in all,
one for each of the twelve tribes of Israel. We will use these
stones to build a memorial. In the future your children will ask
you, 'What do these stones mean?' Then you can tell them,
'They remind us that the Jordan River stopped flowing when
the Ark of the Lord's Covenant went across.' *These stones
will stand as a memorial among the people of Israel forever.*"

Joshua 4:5-7, emphasis added (NLT)

I remember that first day. The first Sunday at church after I had made a very intellectual decision to follow Christ. Like I mentioned before, the moment I decided to follow Jesus, wasn't a grand lightbulb moment, I had been searching for years. Asking questions that rarely got answers. Trying to find someone who could tell me about the Jesus I knew and that my heart was yearning for.

Even though I didn't grow up in church, I knew I would recognize Him once I met Him. Sounds strange I know, but God doesn't need a church building to meet us in. Don't get me wrong, I love the local church. I love fellowship and worshiping together with my church family. But I also know God is not limited to a church building!

As a young girl, I would meet with Jesus in our secret place. Packing up a little bag of snacks, a drink, a book, and my journal, I would set out. Walking down that dusty road behind my house. Climbing through several fences, across grassy fields, and down into the Aussie bush. I would see the odd kangaroo and listen to the kookaburras and parrots singing in the gum trees. Always on the lookout for a snake or two that could be sunbathing in the long grass.

And then I would arrive. At our little pond full of frogs and tadpoles and the occasional blue tongue lizard who would visit. In the shade of the tree, sitting on my rock, I would write and dream with God, often sharing my thoughts and fears. And always knowing He was there with me. No preacher or Bible school teacher taught me who Jesus was. I didn't own a Bible, but I knew Jesus. He was my teacher and my confidante.

Fast forward 20 years, still searching, still seeking. Several pages now of questions, Scriptures, and more questions. And then it happened. A divine appointment while grocery shopping. I noticed the sign 'Christian Church' and decided to go in and ask a question. Mustering up all the courage I could, I proceeded to the church. There was a young man there, whom I assumed was the cleaner, as he didn't have a minister's white collar on. He sat down with me for an hour and chatted with me, offering to come to my house the next evening to answer my pages of questions. Long story short, he came, he answered, and I knew in my heart that this was the Jesus I had been searching for. The same Jesus who met me at that pond all those years ago.

My decision was not based on emotion or even conviction, but rather a recognition deep within my spirit that this man knew the same Jesus I had known all my life. I felt a mixture of relief and deep assurance.

The following Sunday we attended church for the very first time. People seemed genuinely happy! They sang with all their hearts. And the preacher, he described Jesus like He was a real person. I was so excited!

Here I was surrounded by a group of people who knew Jesus. Not some far away God seated on an ethereal throne. But a Jesus, who was real. Who was relatable and who knew me. My heart was ready to explode!

So why am I sharing the story? Because sometimes it's good to remind ourselves of who Jesus is to us. This story is one of my memory stones that build my journey with Christ.

In Joshua 4:5 the Israelites erected memorial stones on the site where they crossed the Jordan River. To remind themselves and future generations of God's miracle.

So too, should we be intentional about building memorial stones in our own walks with God. For ourselves and our future generations. They remind us of who Jesus is. That He can't be put in a box. That He never gives up on us. And of course for myself, reminding me of His faithfulness to a young girl who secretly met with Him in the middle of the Aussie bush.

Author: Kim Beaumont

REFLECTION QUESTIONS

What are some of your memorial stones?

What is your earliest memory of meeting with Jesus?

What can you do to steward your memorial stones?

A Calf Called Hope

Hope deferred makes the heart sick,
But when the desire comes, it is a tree of life.

Proverbs 13:12 (NKJV)

She was our second calf born last spring, right at the beginning of what our family calls the "Coronavirus Chaos." The whole world had turned upside down and inside out; and the kids and I were clinging to any semblance of hope. We hoped that things would return to normal, hoped that we wouldn't get sick, hoped that we would be able to buy toilet paper and coffee the next time we went to the grocery store, and hoped that my husband's work wouldn't come to a screeching halt. We were all sick and tired of facing each day with fear and uncertainty, and what we needed was a little hope to bring light into a darkened time.

The calves came early, and the Wyoming snow and bitter cold stayed later; that combination meant that ears, tails, and feet were susceptible to freezing if we didn't get newborn calves out of the extreme cold and into the house or heated shop. This is what happened to the first two calves born in April. One calf perked right up and looked to be none the worse for wear, we were able to get him out to his mama right away; but that second calf required every bit of effort and ability I had to bring her around.

I dug deep into my memories of the lessons my mother taught me about saving chilled calves. The tiny heifer laid listless in the back of our Ranger in the shop, and for hours I brought heated towels back and forth, trying to bring warmth into her little body. I tubed her with electrolytes to try and get a spark of life out of her. I rubbed her body, her legs, and her nose willing her to keep fighting. I prayed. The kids and I prayed, and I asked friends to pray as well. I never like to lose calves, but this one had become special to me because this one represented hope during an otherwise, hopeless time. I couldn't lose her because I didn't want to lose hope.

Little by little she livened up. We moved her from the shop to the barn where fresh straw and her mama waited. We tried to get her up and nursing, but she couldn't stand on her own; it looked as if one back leg had frozen to the bone. I tubed her again. My husband said not to get my hopes up. Even if she were to live, she would likely lose that back leg and we couldn't let her suffer walking around on a stub. My dad told me it was hopeless as well; once a foot becomes frozen like that, there isn't really anything that can be done to save it. And yet, still I hoped, still I prayed. The kids and I decided to name her "Hope" because that's what we clung to.

Now, almost a year later, when I go out to feed our pen of heifer calves each morning, I am reminded that Hope is alive and well! She is a sweet girl, and quickly becoming one of my favorites. Signs of her battle for life are evident, she's missing the tips of both ears, as well as part of her tail. Occasionally, she walks a little stiff, but Mike and I have been pleasantly encouraged by the fact that her foot seems to be fine and intact. "Hope" shows a lot of promise of growing into a good cow and giving us many years of future calves.

This heifer reminds me that hope isn't always easy to hold onto. Sometimes it takes effort to keep hope fed, warm, and thriving, but hope lives in the unpleasant, uncertain, and unlikely conditions of life. Hope can seem unattainable during difficult circumstances, and I dig deep to find hope so I can face the day with optimism; yet God's Word tells us that hope is more than just mere optimism. Hebrews 10:23 (NKJV) says, "Let us hold fast the confession of our hope without wavering." Hope is described in this verse as," faith, an expectation or a confidence." The key to keeping hope alive is knowing where it's cultivated, knowing where to put our confidence. When we realize the hope that we have is in Christ, and not in the circumstances around us, it's like a tree of life...sweet, satisfying and reviving to our souls. If you want hope to be cultivated in your life, seek God and the hope He brings through faithful confidence in Jesus. If you need a reminder of what hope looks like, think of "Hope," our little Red Angus heifer.

Author: Jana Fraley

REFLECTION QUESTIONS

Can you think of a time when you struggled cultivating in your life?

What do you do when hopes are deferred or disappointed?

Who do you know in your life that is a good reminder of hope?

Nachmu, Nachmu Ami-Comfort, Comfort My People

Comfort, comfort my people, says your God.

Isaiah 40:1 (ESV)

Blessed be the God and Father of our Lord Jesus Christ,
the Father of mercies and God of all comfort, who
comforts us in all our affliction, so that we may be able to
comfort those who are in any affliction, with the comfort
with which we ourselves are comforted by God.

2 Corinthians 1:3-4 (ESV)

When things are going awry in our lives, we believers look to God for hope- hope that our faith will carry us through the tough times and hope to believe God is at work and will teach us much through our trials.

I was in a very dark place because my daughter's son, my 9 year old grandson Caleb was experiencing some severe seizures. My faith in God is especially tested when something happens to my kids and grandkids, even more so than when something happens to me. I spent a lot of time on my knees and with my nose buried in the Bible, seeking help. One day I opened my Bible and out fell a picture that Caleb had given me when he was 4 years old of two eagles sitting on a branch. I turned the picture over and saw that I had written, "Caleb gave me this picture which reminds me that 'They shall mount up with wings like eagles' (Isaiah 40:31, ESV). All of a sudden I felt to turn to that chapter in the Bible: "Comfort, comfort my people, says your God," begins the chapter. I eagerly pulled out my Hebrew Bible and read: "Nachmu, nachmu ami—comfort, comfort my people."

Meanwhile, I had begun making a cross-stitch picture for our son and his fiancée who were getting married that summer. One night I was feeling particularly heavy hearted about Caleb and I decided I should work on the cross-stitch while watching a movie. On a whim, I poked the word "epilepsy" in the Netflix search bar and chose a movie called "Fight For Life." The story had to do with a couple with two children: a 13-year-old son and an 8-year-old daughter. Everything was great in the family until the daughter out of the blue started having grand mal seizures. It turned the family upside down, as it had my daughter's family. I watched and the tears flowed freely from my eyes onto the cross-stitch picture. Life can really be going great one minute and tragedy can strike the next.

The movie continued and the little girl had been given every combination of drugs allowable which had not arrested the seizures at all. Meanwhile, the son of the family was preparing for his Bar Mitzvah, a very important coming of age ceremony for Jewish boys. He wanted his dad to listen to him recite the section of the Bible he was preparing for that event. The dad was in a rush to go back to his daughter who was in the hospital but stopped to listen to his son who picked up his Bible and started chanting in Hebrew, "Nachmu, nachmu ami..." I put my cross-stitch down and stared at the screen. Did I just hear the Hebrew words I had just been reading in Isaiah? Touching music started playing as the camera panned in on the dad, who looked pensively up, as if to God, as if something had just touched him deeply in his heart. I stood up from the couch where I was sitting and fell to my knees and cried and cried. Only God could insert in a movie about epilepsy the very words *in Hebrew* that I had been reading from Isaiah 40 just that week. It seemed impossible but it was so like Him to do what no one else could do, to touch me in my deepest heart , to comfort me in a way that no one else could comfort me. This was the hope I needed. From then on, I became convinced that God was very much involved in Caleb's life, in his situation, in the epilepsy. I didn't need to fear it because He was there. And He is there with you and your loved ones in the darkest night and He knows how to touch you, to comfort you, to meet you in your time of deepest need.

Author: Miriam Kook

REFLECTION QUESTIONS

What situation in your life has ever brought you to your knees?

How has God helped you in difficult situations you have encountered?

Has anyone else's story of God's comforting them brought comfort to you in your time of need?

The Good Shepherd's Work

Jesus said, 'Have the people sit down.' Now there was much grass in the place. So the men sat down, about five thousand in number.'

John 6:11 (ESV)

The week before kindergarten enrollment, my husband came to me with a thought. "What if we homeschool him for a year and see where it goes from there?"

I nervously agreed. I had prayed for this opportunity but felt safe in my husband's "no" because it meant I didn't have to follow through with it. Until I did.

In God's good grace and abundant provision, He equipped me for the call, and I graduated that kid from our homeschool in 2018 and his brother two years later. Sometimes God instructs us to do something that we cannot yet understand. But in the heart of God, it is already a completed work.

In a similar way, those five thousand men and their families who were following Jesus couldn't have understood why they were being told to sit down on the hillside when really the time to eat was drawing near and their stomachs were beginning to rumble. Yet they obeyed. We see no indication in Scripture otherwise. Even more fascinating than their obedience was the place where they sat.

The mountains in the middle east are not typically rolling green hills of grass, but rather barren, rocky land. Verse eleven gives us an indication of something beneath the surface here. It interjects this quiet sentence. "Now there was much grass in the place." Interesting.

Ancient shepherds would have to work to prepare the land ahead of time to have places where they could graze their sheep. Grass growing work was not easy and required forethought, time, and effort. A grassy hill was an indication of a good shepherd having completed a work in order to feed his sheep.

It is almost mind-blowing to realize that Jesus, The Good Shepherd, was giving His sheep instructions to follow that did not make sense, all the while they were sitting in the Shepherd's completed work. Jesus has come to complete the work of salvation for any who would place their faith in Him. As we sit in the completed work, He calls us to tasks that feel far beyond us, hard to understand, and often quite impossible without Him.

I know you're tired and hungry and see no provision, sit down on the grass and rest in My provision. I know you are scared, confused, weary of the trials, and bad news, sit down and rest in My provision and you will find all you need to be satisfied.

Those homeschooling years were not easy, but I held on to the calling and instructions of the Good Shepherd who entrusted the task to me. I cried out to Him and rested often in Him, trusting He would see us through this good work He prepared for us to walk through. All these years later, I am so grateful for having persevered through the task, the provision, and mostly I am grateful for the completed work of the One who makes me lie down in green pastures He has accomplished for me.

Author: Mariel Davenport

REFLECTION QUESTIONS

What has the Good Shepherd called you to, what task is He instructing you to step into?

In what way can you obey and rest while trusting Him to be the provision even when you don't understand?

When I Get Small

Truly I say to you, unless you turn and become like children, you will never enter the kingdom of heaven. Whoever humbles himself like this child is the greatest in the kingdom of heaven.

Matthew 18:3-4 (ESV)

He just couldn't quite see. Even on tiptoe. Those blasted average-height men with watermelon heads kept crowding in front of him. Frustrated, he cursed his small stature for the bazillionth time in his life, and glanced around. Aha! Pushing his way through the dusty swamp of sweaty shoulders, he scaled a tree and clung to the branches, squinting down the road. Yes! There he was! Jesus of Nazareth, the one they called Messiah, coming towards him!

Messiah stopped and looked up. He froze as they made eye contact. In an instant, he felt naked, hanging there on that branch. The contents of his character laid bare between them, he and this Jesus, the one who knew everything he had ever done, and saw through his very soul as though it were made of glass.

"Zacchaeus!" Messiah shouted, "Zacchaeus! Come down!"

I was reminded of little Zacchaeus the other day when the kids and I went to the park for a picnic lunch. The weather was perfect and we were desperate for some fresh air and sunshine, a much-needed change of scenery. It had been forever since I had purposefully taken pictures of anything, so I took my camera along, hoping to get some good shots of the kids. I got more than that.

I've always been captivated by trees. Trees make me feel peaceful and small in the best possible way. I just love the picture: branches reaching for Heaven, roots hidden deep below the soil, drinking in water that can't be seen, but is known by the lush, green leaves clinging to its limbs, soaking up the sun.

Standing there beneath those towering trees, it occurred to me how often I am like Zacchaeus, resenting my smallness. Like him, I have felt the need to somehow overcome my lacking stature by climbing higher, trying to catch a glimpse of something greater. Trying to see. Trying to be seen.

We despise being "small." It's gross near the ground. We scheme and strive to get ourselves up out of the dirt, away from the sweaty crowd and up into the tree where we think we can see more and breathe deeper. But the truth is, those spindly branches near the top are fine and frail and cannot hold our weight. The higher we get, the more danger we're in.

And yet, Jesus calls me down from my precarious position, perched up there on those thin, flimsy branches near the top, and meets me low. On solid ground. Where the dust is.

Throughout the gospels, Jesus frequently admonishes adults to become "like little children," but never once does he tell children to become like adults:

"Truly I say to you, unless you turn and become like children, you will never enter the kingdom of heaven. Whoever humbles himself like this child is the greatest in the kingdom of heaven." Matthew 18:3

This paradoxical Savior turns everything upside down and inside out:

Be gentle to extinguish wrath.

Hold your life tight and you will lose it.

Let go of your life and you will gain it.

The first shall be last.

The last shall be first.

Seek greatness and be brought low.

Seek lowliness and be made great.

And Jesus Himself showed us how. The spotless lamb broke bread with sinners. The hands that formed Adam from the dirt washed the dirt from his disciples' feet. The voice that spoke the earth into existence became a newborn's cry. The king became servant, from throne of glory to animal trough. Jesus came low, and brought us the gift of small.

Small does not carry the weight of the world.

Small does not bear the burden of provision.

Small enjoys the peace of a child along for the ride.

Small feels the joy of being carried along, on the strong, broad shoulders on which the government rests (Isaiah 9:6).

We need not climb the highest tree to grasp at greatness or to be seen by the living God. His kingdom realm is not high in the sky, just out of reach. It is way down low, at the base of the tree. He is waiting there, with dust on His feet, to keep company with us.

"Zacchaeus! Come down! I am coming to your house today!" (Luke 19:10).

Author: Jennifer Hayes

REFLECTION QUESTIONS

What makes you feel "small?"

Does "small" feel good or bad? Why?

Name one way that smallness can be gift in your life.

Ready Your Vessels

Now a certain woman of the wives of the sons of the prophets cried out to Elisha saying, 'Your servant my husband is dead—you know that your servant feared Adonai. Now the creditor has come to take my two children to be his slaves. 'What should I do for you?' Elisha asked her. 'Tell me, what do you have in the house?' She replied, 'Your handmaid has nothing in the house except a jar of oil.' Then he said, 'Go borrow for yourself vessels from all your neighbors—empty jars—not just a few. Then go inside and shut the door behind you and behind your sons and pour into all those vessels, setting aside what is full.' So, she left him and shut the door behind her and behind her sons. They kept bringing the vessels to her and she kept pouring. When the vessels were full, she said to her son, 'Bring me another vessel.' But he said to her, 'There isn't another vessel.' So, the oil stopped.

2 Kings 4:1-7 (TLV)

O ur church entered 2019 about two million dollars in debt. A prophecy had come forth to our church that prompted our pastor to make the decision to be debt free by December 31, 2019. The church underwent a massive cost-cutting campaign to free up money to go toward the debt and a call was made to the congregation to consider helping by way of voluntary financial pledges. I remember the Sunday that the plea went forth. I was sitting next to my mother-in-law as the pastor spoke. He said that anyone who wanted to contribute financially could come up to the front of the sanctuary and pick up a special color-coded envelope based on the amount of pledge we were making. Immediately the spirit prompted me to go forth and get an envelope even though my husband was not there to discuss the decision with. My mother-in-law went with me and we both returned with blue envelopes in our hands. As I sat and wondered how I would keep the commitment that I had just made, I felt the Lord reassure me that He would provide. Not only would He provide, but it would be from my hands and not our household budget. So that envelope went home with me. I had brought my vessel behind closed doors and now it was time for the Lord to let the oil begin to pour.

Within one week, I received two checks from medical providers for significant amounts. One had a memo with it that advised me that I had overpaid my bill. Now really, who overpays their doctor bill? I had paid exactly what they had billed me, but I realized then that the Lord had been preparing the oil in advance for me. I also cashed in a large jar of change I had been saving at home. I sold some clothes at a consignment shop. I skipped my weekly chai tea latte and cut back on eating lunch out. Before I knew it, and well ahead of schedule, my envelope was filled and my pledge commitment was fulfilled. Like the widow woman, I kept gathering more jars and pouring oil and the Lord kept multiplying what I had in my hands until the last vessel was full.

The interesting thing to me is that before I made the pledge, I did not have that extra money. But as soon as I got my vessel ready and made my pledge to the Lord, the oil began to flow and He provided the way to fill my jars. When the jar was full because my pledge was complete, the oil stopped flowing. Another key point is that I never doubted that God would provide. What need do you have today that seems impossible to fill? Like I did, get your expectations up, kick doubt out the door, and get your vessels ready in anticipation of God meeting your need.

To take this one step further, God also wants to fill you up with His Spirit and His anointing so that you can be poured out into the lives of others to bring Him glory. Our mission in life is to make Him known and to bring Him glory. Just like writing this devotional and the others I have in this book, until I sat down and got myself ready at my computer to write, until I made a demand on the Spirit, the oil did not flow. But once I sat down and said, "Alright Lord, here I am. Use me!" The oil of His Word began to flow, the words began to take shape on the page and in no time at all, my commitment to this book was complete. So, do not shrink back when you hear the voice of The Lord saying, "Make a pledge, step out into ministry, bless someone with a gift, write that book." Whatever that thing is that God has been asking you to do, make a demand on the Spirit. Step out in faith. Ready your vessels and watch the oil begin to flow.

Author: Anita Stafford

REFLECTION QUESTIONS

Have you ever felt led to make a financial pledge or commitment to a ministry? What happened? Did you step out in faith? How did God meet your need?

Jesus, Friend to the Outcast

The Lord appeared to me (Israel) from ages past,
saying, 'I have loved you with an everlasting love;
therefor, with lovingkindness, I have drawn you
and continued My faithfulness to you.

Jeremiah 31:3 (AMP)

From the time I was a young child, I was already drawn to encouragement and defending the underdog, the outcast, ones left behind, forgotten, and bullied. I was incredibly triggered by any type of violence or injustice on TV, even in the form of a cartoon. The first time I recall defending an outcast was in the 7th grade. Rather than use my voice to stand in the gap for the timid victim in my school gym room, I recoiled with like-minded behavior, and looking back, I may still have chosen that route in hindsight. It got the point across, that not everyone is going to accept injustice with silence. There will be people brave enough to step up in defense and befriend the unfriended.

Jesus led such a beautiful example of this all throughout the Gospel. Lepers, outcasts, Gentiles, and Greeks, prostitutes, adulteresses, tax collectors, and every other disreputable child of God. Christ was at the center of humanity, and felt at home in every setting, except a hypocritical temple, slapping a whitewash paintbrush over their hatred. He stood between the woman caught in the act of adultery and her accusers, bringing their arrogance in line with their sin-filled hearts, and even they couldn't find cause to cast the first stone. One by one, they turned tail and walked away, leaving Jesus with her one broken heart.

When I was a teenager, I was painfully aware of the fact that I was not even a third wheel. I was along for the ride simply to be a comic relief in any given situation. Although it was second nature for me to jump to the defense of a child being bullied, I simply didn't have the courage, or the self-worth, to do it for myself. I would rather be at the receiving end of a practical joke than be excluded and disregarded. These painful memories have given me insight into the sad truths around bullied children. Those children who believe they are worthless and wouldn't know acceptance if it fell on their faces, are generally the ones willing to sit through a bullying session. Apparently, I was one of these, and didn't realize it until I was several years into my marriage and still battling low self-worth.

When I was 12 years old, I went to Target with my two closest friends. We were 600 miles away from home on a gymnastics competition and I was feeling particularly sensitive to the behavior. While shopping for the latest style of sports pants, I found myself alone, in a place which felt overwhelmingly far from home. My friends and I found three pair of matching pants, two blue and one red. We were negotiating over who would be the oddball, when I turned around to find a pair of red pants lying at my feet and no friends in sight. They ran to a checkout, and by the time I found them, they were waiting at the entrance with a very irritated chaperone. To this day, I still despise the color red. This type of behavior continued throughout the trip, and when I was dropped off at home (first, I might add) I was painfully reminded that I was second best, and the source of several bouts of laughter.

As I mentioned earlier, I have carried this into my marriage, and every subsequent friendship of my adult life. Silence speaks louder than words, and I often find myself emphatically apologizing for things when a friend goes silent, just to ensure I am still wanted, still needed, still valuable. I will cause myself to bend and contort if I feel it will strengthen the bond. I will lose sleep, overthinking every word and comma, and be certain they will eventually abandon me.

This morning, I came across this verse from 1 Corinthians 4:3 (NLT) "As for me, it matters very little how I might be evaluated by you or any human authority. I don't even trust my own judgment on this point." It spoke so clearly to me, that while it is important to live like Christ, loving our friends as Christ loves the church, it is not for me to seek approval from the world, or myself.

I don't know how long it'll take to believe this in the core of my being, but it's a step in the right direction, and one I know I must take. I need to love, not to ensure I won't be abandoned, but to be a vessel for Christ. It is okay if I am not loved by every soul I know. It's okay to be yourself and it's okay if not everyone loves you. Jesus' opinion of me is far more important than the world's. I'm not there yet, but by His grace, I can leave behind people pleasing, and press into living unapologetically authentic, and so can you. You are beloved. You are worth your weight in gold. And you were born for such a time as this.

Author: Kristin Cash

REFLECTION QUESTIONS

Have you known Jesus as a friend when others have abandoned you?

What are some ways you have reached out to be the peace-bearing hands of Christ?

Have you dealt with past trauma in friendship? Have you shared in safe circles?

The Way that I Should Go

This is what the Lord says – your Redeemer, the Holy One of Israel: 'I am the Lord your God, who teaches you what is best for you, who directs you in the way you should go.'

Isaiah 48:17 (NIV)

For years I used to agonize over knowing God's will for my life. When I had a decision to make, I would think through all the pros and cons. I would make lists with columns–for and against under each choice. Should I go live here? Should I take this job? Which choice is the right one? What path is the one that keeps me in God's will? The prevailing thinking in the church at the time was that there was one right path that was God's best plan for your life. You needed to figure out what that path was and if you made a mistake, then you were stuck with God's second best for the rest of your life.

Even as I write these words, I see that this narrow view of God's will shows an equally narrow view of God. It pictures Him as uncaring, as sitting up in Heaven with all these plans for us and just waiting for us to guess correctly. I no longer see God that way. I see a God who loves me overwhelmingly! And yet, even as I learned more about His love for me, I still wondered how to discern His will. How do I know if I am on the right path or not?

This verse in Isaiah has been a favorite one of mine for many years now. It tells me that God is not just sitting up in Heaven hoping that I will choose His best plan for me. It says that God will actually teach me what is best for me. This isn't just what is best in a general sense, but what is best for me personally. And I don't need to flounder around wondering which way I should go. This verse says that He will direct me in the way I should go.

Since God showed me this verse, it has given me so much comfort. It's not that I suddenly knew exactly what to do when I was needing direction in my life. And I have needed direction often because of the path that God has had me on in life. I have lived many places, had many jobs and places to live, so I have needed God's direction for those decisions repeatedly over the years. But this verse assured me that God was there in each decision, wanting to teach me, willing to direct me. That gave me peace.

How does this play out in my life? When I talk with someone about this, I usually use the phrase, "Knock on the door." The visual that comes to me when I am needing to decide about a change in my life is that there is one door or perhaps multiple doors ahead of me. I move in a particular direction and ask God to direct by either opening the door or keeping it closed. If it opens, I move through it. If it remains closed, I knock on another door. Sometimes moving through the one open door is all that is needed. Sometimes it leads to another choice, another door.

Choosing to live like this, to knock on doors and move through the open ones, has given me a perspective of how God directs me. I see Him as the One who gives me opportunities, the One who is in control of the doors in my life. I see Him using these doors to direct me in the way I should go, as Isaiah said. He is teaching me what is best for me as He directs me. I admit that I don't always remember this in the pressure of making a decision.

A few years ago, I was deliberating between whether to stay at the place I was working or move to a new one. I was feeling quite stressed about how to know which would be best and expressed that to my roommate. She immediately prayed that God would make it very clear to me what I was supposed to do. When I got to work that day, I found out that someone was leaving, and I was being offered a different position that had all the pros of the potential new place of employment with the security that came with the current place. God answered my roommate's prayer immediately and made my decision very clear. He doesn't always answer that quickly or that clearly. But I have found that as I move forward, knock on doors, and then wait for His leading, He has taught me to see His direction more readily.

Author: Barb Loewen

REFLECTION QUESTIONS

In what way does this verse from Isaiah change your view of how God wants to lead you?

What doors are in front of you that you could trust God to open or leave closed, if you just knock?

Are there doors in your life that you keep banging on, trying to force open, when God has kept them closed? How can you submit and trust Him with that?

Turning to the One with the Answer

Cast your burden upon the Lord and he will sustain you. He will never allow the righteous to be shaken.

Psalm 55:22 (NLT)

I woke up this morning with that familiar pit in my stomach that I have unfortunately come to recognize. Sometimes I'm still trying to figure out what triggers it. Often, it's painfully obvious, like the year we lost our son, Cody.

But now as I dwell on that feeling, I realize it's been there most of my life. At some time or another. An emptiness and restlessness that tries to take hold and render me powerless. If I allow myself to succumb, it continues to torment me through my thoughts and eventually my feelings. Bringing anxiety and fear to whatever is my current worry or area of concern. And of course there is always something, that's just a fact of life.

I used to wonder: *Is this just me?* It's certainly not something that people chat about around the dinner table. Over the years I learned I have a choice. I can entertain the thoughts, the what if's, the buts, and the maybes. Or I can turn my heart and my mind towards the only one who has the answers. The One who often answers the questions I haven't even thought of yet.

Sometimes I can identify the root behind the gnawing feeling in my gut. But often, I cannot. I can spiritualize it and put a name to it. Or psychoanalyze it and define the condition. However, for me, I don't think it deserves a title. Bottom line, it is not who I am. It is not my identity and it does not control me.

1 John 4:4 "Greater is He who is in me than he is in the world." I cannot and will not ever forget this truth. And I know no matter how I'm feeling, or what is happening in my world, that one truth never changes. Because of that I can choose to focus my attention on the One who has the answers and the One who always strengthens me in my weakness.

I love Joyce Meyer's take on Proverbs 23:7. *'The man goes where the mind follows.'* Learning to recognize what I am thinking about, dwelling upon, and feeding myself has been key in conquering those feelings and thoughts that try to overwhelm me. Feelings make wonderful servants, but are terrible masters.

I want to encourage you today. No matter what is happening in your life. There is someone greater than your biggest problem or your deepest fear that you can turn to! His heart is for you. He's not afraid of mess and He's waiting for you with open arms to reach out to Him. His name is Jesus. He knows exactly how you're feeling, and He is there to carry your burden. Why not give Him a try today? What have you got to lose?

Romans 12:2 (NIV)

"Do not conform to the pattern of this world, but be transformed by the renewing of your mind. Then you will be able to test and approve what God's will is—his good, pleasing and perfect will."

Author: Kim Beaumont

REFLECTION QUESTIONS

When you have that gnawing feeling, what is the first thing you can do to start addressing it?

What is one of your truth's that He has given you?

The Right Kind of Fear

The secret of the Lord is with those who fear Him, and He will show them His covenant. My eyes are ever toward the Lord, for He shall pluck my feet out of the net.

Psalm 25:14-15 (NKJV)

My 12-year-old son, Kade, is obsessed with traps of any kind. He has live traps set up all over our ranch, mainly meant to trap the pesky racoons that get in the barn and eat the grain. Several times I've had to rescue an unsuspecting chicken or a curious cat from a trap he has set. We're always on the lookout for any "booby traps" he has hidden to ensnare us as well as an eye out for his swinging rope to be suddenly thrown at our feet. My son is always trying to catch the rest of us in his traps, and I've become proficient at learning how to avoid them.

He and I had a great discussion one day after church. I asked, "What's one thing that stood out to you in today's sermon?" He replied, "That God is scary!" He went on to say, "When the Pastor shared with us how important it is to fear the right thing, what does that mean? What's the right thing to fear?"

I replied, "God. God is the right thing we should be fearing." He rubbed his head, "This is so confusing! God is scary and that's a good thing?" he asked.

"No, I said, it's not that God is scary, it's that God is Awesome, and that inspires us to have a holy fear of Him, and that is the right kind of fear!"

You might be asking the same thing, how can fear of God be a good thing? Several times throughout the Bible we're told to "fear the Lord." And yet we're also told to rest in, trust, and have faith in Him. How do we reconcile fearing God with loving God? What is it about fear that produces trust and rest when what we know about fear results in anxiety and despair?

First, we need to understand the correct meaning of the word "fear" used in the text. This fear is a respectful, reverential, devoted fear that comes from a place of submission, humility, and adoration. It's the type of fear we should have when we're walking with Christ and growing in our faith. When we have this kind of fear of God, He allows us to see a little more clearly what He is doing and understand why. It's a fear that brings wisdom and understanding.

I always think about the part in "The Lion, The Witch, and the Wardrobe"[2] when Susan and Mr. Beaver talk about the lion, Aslan; "'Is he quite safe? I shall feel rather nervous about meeting a lion'...'Safe?' said Mr. Beaver...'Who said anything about safe? 'Course he isn't safe. But he's good. He's the King, I tell you.'" This is what I know to be true about fearing God; He isn't safe, but He is oh so good! God intends for His awesome power and holiness to be fearful, not to drive us away from Him, but to draw us toward Him.

This kind of fear isn't terror. Those who are walking in opposition or rebellion to Him might experience terror when they think of God; and they should because He isn't to be trifled with, mocked, or scorned. He is holy and can't be associated with sin of any kind. There are consequences to rebellion, and that should terrify us. But once we have experienced salvation, redemption, and regeneration, we are free from terror.

What do we do when the cares, concerns, and worries of this world begin to entangle us, when we find ourselves suddenly caught in a net of fear? Just like the traps that my son sets around our ranch, we must be wise and alert to avoid getting caught up in them. Traps either of our own making, or nets of deceit, dishonor, hostility, malice, envy, or greed thrown at us by others. How do we escape the net of our own sin or hostility from enemies? We turn our eyes toward the Lord, keeping our focus on Him and not our worldly fears; our lives become a constant prayer, and our desire is for continual fellowship with Him. God is the one who rescues us from the pit, the trap, and the net that entangles us and holds us captive. On our own we tend to tangle ourselves up more; but when our eyes are always on Him, looking for His daily support and supply, we find escape from those pesky traps in life.

Author: Jana Fraley

REFLECTION QUESTIONS

Have you ever felt trapped by fear; if so, how did you escape?

Does it make sense to you that fear can be a good thing?

Do you have a reverential kind of fear of God or a terrified kind of fear?

Intentional Pondering

But Mary treasured up all these things,
pondering them in her heart.

Luke 2:19 (ESV)

Putting together a large puzzle takes time, persistence and determination. My mom came to live with us for a couple months following her hip surgery that had gone array. In that time, she spent several days putting together a new puzzle. It had been a gift for her mind to focus on something other than the healing, the time, and the pain.

As she and I sat at the table sorting and fitting tiny pieces together, it occurred to me how dependent we were on the box top picture. Without the big picture, we had no clue how these tiny picture parts fit together. Why are so many of the pieces cut into such similar shapes?

Every time I pulled together a set of pieces that seemed to fit, I had to look back at the top to determine if I was even aiming in the right direction. It felt parallel to my life.

My Dad passed away after a very brief battle with cancer, leaving a gaping hole in the heart of our small, close-knit family. That puzzle piece of grief was blurry; even now, a year later with my mom's recovery at hand. How is it the pieces of our life feel so out of sorts at times? It often seems that we are handed puzzle pieces, without the box lid.

Luke tells in his gospel of how Mary dealt with this same lack of clarity when handed pieces that made no sense in the present moment. "Mary treasured up all these things, pondering them in her heart."

She was intentional to notice the moments though she lacked clarity; she knew they were significant. When shepherds found her cuddling her newborn Son in a cave with a man she was betrothed to, she pondered. When her Son was lost and then found questioning the rabbis at the temple decades older than Himself because He was to be about His Father's business, she pondered. She lacked a grasp on fully understanding these difficult moments. Yet she trusted God enough to rest in His grace and ponder up the small puzzle pieces He gave her.

Author: Mariel Davenport

REFLECTION QUESTIONS

How can you and I take a moment to treasure up and ponder our moments?

Rather than live in fear or anxiety in the trials, what if we gave thanks for who God is in them and treasured the moment, knowing one day when we see Him face to face, we will know the big picture and it will all make sense?

When the Limp is the Gift

Your name will no longer be Jacob, but Israel, because you have struggled with God and humans and have overcome.

Genesis 32:28 (NIV)

It was a Friday in September of sixth grade when I came home from school with a sore hip. By Sunday night I was in such agonizing pain that when my dad brushed against the bed and jiggled it, I screamed. By Monday morning, I was in emergency surgery to drain a septic infection from my hip joint before it reached my blood stream. I was eleven.

What had caused this mysterious infection?

It took two long, agonizing, frustrating years to finally get a diagnosis. Juvenile Rheumatoid Arthritis. I spent the rest of my teens in and out of hospitals, physio appointments, blood tests, and two more surgeries.

Friendships were hard. Other kids passed notes in class. I couldn't hold a pencil. They had track and field. I could barely walk. They had plans. I had appointments. They had dates. I had a cane and a limp.

Genesis 32 tells us that Jacob "wrestled" with God. Here the Hebrew word for "wrestled" is "abaq," which means, "to float away like a vapor or particles of light; to grapple; to bedust (get dusty)."

Jacob was wrestling with God, and with himself. His need to control, to manipulate outcomes, and people, to be independent, to come out ahead. He struggled to submit to God, to His plans, to His outcomes, to His presence. When Jacob wrestled with God there on the banks of Jabbok, he wasn't just wrestling with his own frailty, he was literally wrestling with the very *substance of God Himself. With* the dust. *In* the dust. *All through the night.*

When God touched Jacob's hip, he put it out of joint and gave him a life-long limp. So, Jacob did what we all must do. He surrendered. *And then God blessed him* (v. 29). It took the limp to convince Jacob of his need for God. Without it, Jacob would have continued in his own determination, far from the purpose and presence of the One who formed him and called him by name. But with the limp came surrender, and through surrender, *blessing.* When Jacob wrestled with God, he saw him *face to face.* The struggle brings us *low,* but it also brings us *close.*

Hobbling through my youth with a literal limp, I can sympathize with Jacob. This determined, self-reliant, get-it-done girl had a long road ahead of learning the beautiful art of surrender, convinced that long-suffering meant relentless striving. At a young age, I learned the painful, but precious truth of my profound need for God. My daily struggle with physical pain in my hands, feet, hips, gave me a taste of Christ's suffering for my sake. Pain is the holy portal through which we behold Him and become like Him. *Pain is how we see Him face-to-face.* Like Jacob, my limp was my place of blessing. *My limp was a gift.*

When we wrestle with God in the dirt, grappling with the dust of our inadequacies, in between those particles is also light. We can't grapple in the dust without also touching the glory of God, the sum and substance of His character, the presence of His love and light. *This is holy ground. This is where the blessing is.*

Where once my limp made me an *outsider,* it now makes me an *along-sider.* I used to get left *behind,* but now I can stay *beside.* Because of my limp, I have had extraordinary opportunities to bear witness to the miraculous work of God in the hard places of others. I can sit with them there in the dark, in the dust of their pain, and have a sacred conversation. I can offer the light I have grasped through my own struggle. The light of compassion. The light of presence. The light of understanding. The light of hope. This too is holy ground. This too is where blessing is.

In my early adulthood, against all medical odds, God did heal my body, but the scar on my hip is an ever-present reminder of my ever-present need for my ever-present Father. It reminds me also of other scars. Scars in the hands, feet, and side of the One who gave His life for the dust, and healing for the limp.

Read more of Jacob's story in Genesis 25:19-34, and chapters 27-35.

Author: Jennifer Hayes

REFLECTION QUESTIONS

Where in your life have you wrestled with God? Where is your "limp?"

Where can you see the light of God's presence in your grappling?

What is the gift your limp is bringing you?

What sacred conversations can you have because of your limp?

My Dear Daughter

'For I know the plan that I have in mind for you,' declares Adonai, 'plans for shalom and not calamity—to give you a future and a hope. Then you will call on Me, and I will listen to you. You will seek Me and find Me when you will search for me with all your heart. Then I will be found by you' says Adonai...

Jeremiah 29:11-14a (TLV)

A couple of years ago, I reached an exceptionally low point in my life. I was working full-time and had my hands overflowing with issues both at work and home. Like many women, I was taking care of everyone else but not myself. I was so very tired, mentally, physically, and emotionally.

Earlier that year, I had made a commitment to myself and God that I was going to be more consistent with my devotion time. This Saturday morning, I read my devotional study and the Scriptures, but when I was done, I still felt empty. I cried out to God. "Lord, I'm taking care of everyone else, but who is taking care of me? Do you see me? Do you care about what is happening to me right now?"

So very gently and with no hesitation on His part, these words began to drop into my spirit. With the anointing of a scribe, I immediately began to type His words into the notes on my iPad. As the tears flowed, tears of gratitude and thankfulness, the peace of God began to flow over me like warm oil. Since this event, I have been able to share these words with others and they never fail to bring healing where healing is needed, in the heart of a woman.

"I am preparing you for something far greater than you have now, far greater than where you are physically and spiritually. Draw closer to Me, keep in touch with Me. When I say move... move. When I say speak... speak. If it does not come from Me, avoid it. You will need to be laser focused on Me and what I have called you to do. The things that are important to Me should be important to you; souls and letting my people know how much I love them and want to bless them. Don't get discouraged, for in due time I will lift you up. You are my example of obedience and persistence and courage. I will reward you for your hard work. I have already given you everything that you could ever need or want. It is already yours. Call on Me, seek Me, find Me in those moments when you feel alone, lonely, misunderstood, or ignored. You are important to Me. There are things that I need you to do, things that I created you alone for. You are unique and gifted. Created to be My handmaiden on the earth, My message in the flesh, a Godly example of a virtuous woman. So that is where the enemy will attack your thoughts. Stand firm, seek Me, especially when you sense the draw of the enemy. I am for you. Who can be against you? You are more than a conqueror because I am with you. Don't give up. Don't be fearful. Don't lose heart. I will not let you down. My promises are unbreakable by Me. Stay the course and you will see blessings that you did not anticipate and did not dream would happen. And I created you to dream big, so do that too! I love you with a love that took Me to the cross. Never forget that! It is the core of who I am and My love for you. Be strong and courageous. I will lead you to the land of my promises, to the place of abundance and provision. That need that you feel, that desire, I will fill it or remove it if it is not from Me. But keep your eyes on Me, don't look away, don't let go of My hand. Like a child with her Daddy, cling to me for your security and safety. I know what you need and want. Those things that cause you to cry in the middle of the night when no one hears. I hear! I know! Come to Me. Bring them to Me. Let Me hold you as you cry and let Me wipe away those tears. Then let Me remind you of My promises to you. I am always here! I am the Great I Am, the All Sufficient One! Everything you need, Your Provider, and the Lover of your soul! Seek Me. Find Me. Follow Me. I won't let you down, ever! I know what my plans are for you and they are good ones. I am so excited to show you. Stick with Me! This is gonna be good! I have already started you down the path I have planned for you and you did not even realize that My hand was on it. Now you will begin to see Me at work. Watch for the God moments in every day. I love you! I love you! I love you! You are precious to Me!

Author: Anita Stafford

REFLECTION QUESTIONS

Have you ever felt alone as though no one cared about you?

Do you have a personal relationship with Christ? If not, please know that He loves you, cares about you and is waiting for you. It is as simple as telling God that you accept Him as your Lord and Savior and want Him to take charge of your life. You can pray that simple prayer right now!

Finding Jesus in the Deep Dive

When you go through rivers of difficulty, you will not drown. When you walk through the fire of oppression, you will not be burned up; the flames will not consume you.

Isaiah 43:2 (NLT)

There are moments in life which can best be described as deep diving, when waves of grief, uncertainty, fear, changes in our plans, careers, or childrearing can plummet us beneath the surface of the water. Down there, where we are utterly powerless, we are entirely at the mercy of the force of the waves.

Did you know that the average wave, 4 foot in height, 10 seconds in strike, puts out more than 35,000 horsepower per mile of coast? That is an intense amount of force on one helpless body.

Helpless, yes. But, not hopeless. It is in these moments of powerlessness that we learn what our faith is made of? Did we use hay, sticks, or bricks in the construction of our faith-home? Deep diving with Jesus is a surefire way to expose the stuff our lives are made of.

Most of us might be willing to admit that we have had more than our fair share of deep diving lessons. I am no different. But, in hindsight, when given the opportunity to discern my reaction to certain circumstances, I crave these true grit moments with my Savior. It is the feeling of release, settling into the nook and cradle of His embrace, and taking in a full, deep breath, while letting God do what only He can do.

Flailing about will only cause us harm. Resisting and striving will only draw us further into the deep. But the idea of grabbing hold of Jesus, diving beneath the surface of the situation, while clinging tightly to Him, is the only tangible thing we can trust in those moments. Jesus will prove Himself faithful, trustworthy, wise, and steadfast. He will teach us the muscle memory needed to become victorious; to rise to the surface unscathed.

In 2014, my husband came home, days before the mortgage was due, and told me that he felt led to go into business for himself. I asked exactly what he meant by this, and he told me he would be giving a two week notice to his boss the next morning, and starting his own handyman company with a handful of customers. Beginning a construction company, with little to no support, felt like I was being drawn beneath the waves; deeper with every breath, and the feeling of hopelessness rising within me.

But, after a few days had passed, I began to dream of what the future might hold for our family, and awaken to the idea that we weren't being forgotten by a good God with a gracious plan. I embraced the feeling of holding onto Jesus while He shielded me from the tumult of my surroundings. I felt held, and for the first time in many years, I knew the powerful yet gentle embrace of my Savior, and I knew we were exactly where He wanted us to be.

The future was uncertain, but only to our limited perception. I had to ask for a Heavenly vantage point. It wasn't that God was punishing me for being made of flesh, full of doubts and uncertainty, rather He was teaching me that His plans were worth the momentary discomforts.

I won't begin to sugarcoat things, and paint a serene picture of something resembling a Mary Poppins' watercolor. It was wave after wave of redirection, course correction, and reprioritizing. But what came of it has been such a beautiful, one-of-a-kind gift, handcrafted by The Master Craftsmen. That little handyman company is now a thriving General Contracting LLC. with employees and growing contracts. It means no boss to answer to, holidays, birthdays, and vacations without the stress of obligation, and the ability for our children to apprentice under his trades.

Because my husband took a leap of faith, and I was willing to see God's hand at work, I could trust the process, even when it felt dark, tumultuous, and quiet. The quiet was the most unsettling part of being in the deep with Jesus, because I had grown so accustomed to listening to the world instead of waiting on the Lord. Thank God, He is graciously patient with me in my baby steps towards deeper connection with Him.

Author: Kristin Cash

REFLECTION QUESTIONS

What are some moments of deep diving in your life?

Have you felt the nearness of Christ during those times?

How might you help someone who is struggling in their deep dive?

When We are Dust

As a father has compassion on his children, so the Lord has compassion on those who fear him. For he knows how we are formed, he remembers that we are dust.

Psalm 103:13-14 (NIV)

"Is this the best you can do, God?" I was angry! I had been serving God for years, faithfully working in ministry for Him. I had been asking for something which He continued to deny me. What I wanted wasn't that difficult for Him to provide, but He continued to say no. Then He took away a home that I loved and moved me into a tiny place. It wasn't fair as far as I was concerned. I deserved better for my life of service! My anger was justified!

That was what I was feeling. By God's grace, I didn't stay there in that place of anger for a long time. Instead, my feelings of anger soon began to change to feelings of guilt. I was reminded of all that God had done for me. The Father had given His Son as a sacrifice for my sin. The Son had given up His home in Heaven to come to earth to die in my place. The Lord had done these things because He loved me, so that I could accept the free gift of salvation and spend eternity with Him. I didn't deserve this gift. I certainly didn't deserve whatever it was that I thought God owed me for my service. What I deserved was death and hell for the sinfulness of my heart. But instead, I was given adoption into God's family. And the giving didn't stop there. God may not have answered the specific prayer that I had been praying for years, but He had given me many blessings.

As the anger I had been feeling gave way to guilt, I expected God's wrath. That was what I should have received. His message to me should have been one of anger for my self-righteous sense of entitlement. But what He whispered to my heart as the guilt replaced the anger were the words, "He remembers that we are dust." I could hear Him saying to me, "It's okay, Child. I understand."

I was working at a Bible camp at the time, and it was summer—our busiest time. I didn't have time to deal with all that was going on in my heart. But when I was able to get away for a weekend, I looked for those words about dust. I knew they were in the Scriptures, but I didn't know where. My concordance provided the answer—Psalm 103. And I found there, not only the words He had whispered to me, but so many other verses of comfort as well, verses about forgiveness, healing, redemption, love, and compassion. And that was just in the first five verses. It went on to tell me more.

"He does not treat us as our sins deserve or repay us according to our iniquities" (vs 10). Instead, "as far as the east is from the west, so far has he removed our transgressions from us" (vs 12).

And then the verse telling of His compassion, that He knows I am merely dust.

Adam was created from the dust of the ground, formed into the likeness of God, and brought to life by the breath of God (Gen 2:7). God remembers how we were created, and He graciously reminded me of that instead of raining down fire on my head. I deserved the fire, not the grace. But God doesn't give us what we deserve. We couldn't survive if He did. In fact, life wouldn't be worth living if we truly got what we deserve.

I am so grateful that God didn't give me what I deserved that summer. I thank Him always for giving me His grace instead.

Author: Barb Loewen

REFLECTION QUESTIONS

What do you think you deserve from God?

How do you guard against a sense of entitlement?

Where do you go in Scripture when you need to remember God's grace?

Divine Exchange

Come to me, all you who labor and are heavy laden
and I will give you rest. Take my yoke upon you
and learn from me, for I am gentle and lowly of
heart, and you will find rest for your souls.

Matthew 11:28-29 (NKJV)

I remember the first time I ever heard this verse. I didn't even know it was in the Bible. Being new to the faith, my days of learning and valuing Bible promises were still ahead of me.

One morning in church, a girl began to sing, 'Come to me, all you who are heavy laden and I will give you rest.' Initially, it was her voice and the melody that drew my attention. And then her words as she sang them over and over began to touch my heart, deeply. So much so that 25 years later I can still see her and hear her singing those words as they ministered to me and continue to do so till this day.

This is the beauty and power of God's truth. Not only does it pierce through our soul; exposing our fears, our worries, and our false mindsets, but also the lies that we are believing are made plain. Francis Frangipane says, *'If there is any area in your life where you have no hope, you are believing a lie.'*

His truth brings light into the darkness that can hold us captive.

Sometimes we don't even realize we are prisoners functioning in our own personal prison of lies that we're believing as truth. That's the thing about lies and deception. Like a frog in a pot of slow boiling water. When we're in it, we don't even realize it. And slowly, the life in us is being drained away as we paddle and gasp for air, just like that frog.

Not only does His truth reveal the deception, God replaces that lie with a life-giving eternal truth. There is a 'divine exchange' that takes place when we cast our burdens on Him and take up His yoke. God in His mercy not only takes it away, but replaces it with something even better!

Sometimes it's rest, a supernatural rest that can only come from Heaven. Sometimes it's joy, He turns our mourning into dancing. Often it is a peace, a peace that surpasses all understanding of anything we're trying to figure out. But always there is a level of freedom that undergirds that divine exchange when we choose to give it to Him.

"For whom the son sets free is free indeed" (John 8:36, NLT) and that includes you and me! God is so good! His exchanges are always better than we expect. More than we could ever hope, dream, or imagine! If only we would trust Him in the process.

Are you ready for a divine exchange today? I know I am!

Author: Kim Beaumont

REFLECTION QUESTIONS

What do you need to exchange today?

What burden can you give Him in exchange for His rest or peace or joy?

Ask Him what truth promise is He wanting to give to you right now?

I Am My Mother's Daughter

For I will turn their mourning to joy, will comfort them, and make them rejoice rather than sorrow.

Jeremiah 31:13 (NKJV)

It was a beautiful day; the warm Wyoming sun shining on my face, a slight breeze whispering in my ear, walking along a well-worn trail with my mom's dog, "Whitt," following along. This was the kind of day my mother loved. We'd often walk these cow trails together, enjoying deep conversations about life, faith, and family. We'd look for "treasures" like an old tin can, unique rocks, or beautiful wildflowers; all while breathing in the beauty of God's creation.

But today I didn't appreciate the sunshine or the breeze. The silence was palpable and heavy; at once comforting, but also suffocating. I didn't know what I wanted or needed right then; was it to embrace the quietness of the hills and valleys of my parents' remote ranch, or to go back to the house where friends and family were beginning to gather and would envelop me in their well-intentioned, but overwhelming love? The weariness of grief was just beginning to hit me like a tidal wave.

It's crazy how quickly life can change. A week earlier, my family had all been together at my parent's ranch to help with their annual branding. This is always a lot of hard work, but also a wonderful time of food, fellowship, and fun with family and neighbors. A few days after I returned home, my sweet Mom woke up early, had her Quiet Time and a cup of coffee, fed my Dad breakfast, caught her horse, and proceeded to spend the day like a thousand others before: working cattle alongside her husband and son. Shortly after climbing up in the saddle, she was taken from us; dying instantly as her horse fell over backwards, landing on top of her.

Now I was walking the path of grief; and in the days and months to follow, I had to make the decision whether that path would lead me to God or away from Him. Would I allow my grief to define me or refine me? Was I going to escape grief by any means possible, or would I lean into God and walk through it to the other side? Nothing about this heavy sadness was easy, but I found blessing in the refining process that God allowed through it. I learned that the Lord does bring joy in the midst of our mourning, we can find comfort in the most unexpected places, and the truth that it is possible to rejoice even as we are experiencing our deepest sorrows.

We each will face grief at some point in our lives. Some people seem to face more than seems humanly possible to handle. I'll never forget the first time I witnessed the raw pain death leaves; I was a young girl when friends of our family lost their baby girl from a heart condition. This wouldn't be the last child they would bury, a few years later they would lose another baby girl to the same condition.

I remember the way the family's grief affected me, how it kept me up at night wondering how they were going to face the days to come. I can still hear the words my Mom said to me as I sat and cried in my bedroom, my young heart trying to process this loss. She said, "Jana, I know this hurt feels so overwhelming and dark right now, but soon it will fade into a dull ache. And we don't grieve as some people grieve. We grieve with hope; the hope of Heaven that colors all of the darkness with the beautiful light of Jesus."

This was the reminder I clung to as I mourned the death of my Mother; I didn't grieve like one without hope. I had the hope of Heaven and knew I would someday see her there, probably sitting at Jesus' feet, just soaking in His presence. This is the reminder we can all cling to as we face any kind of loss because there is always a grieving process that follows loss. The hope of Jesus colors over the darkness of grief. We recognize that the things of this world are fleeting and finite, but the things of Heaven are eternal and infinite.

Heaven is a sure and certain promise for those who have found forgiveness for their sins and salvation from sin's consequence through Jesus. My own personal journey in grief has brought a greater appreciation for Who the

Lord is and the hope He has given me. Grief was not wasted, my tears and hurt were not in vain. God uses it all to draw us closer to Him.

Author: Jana Fraley

REFLECTION QUESTIONS

Have you experienced the refining process through grief?

Do you know what it means that we don't have to "grieve as one without hope"?

What lessons has God taught you through loss of any kind in your life?

The Ferocious Dog

Be sober-minded; be watchful. Your adversary the devil
prowls around like a roaring lion, seeking someone to
devour. Resist him, firm in your faith, knowing that
the same kinds of suffering are being experienced
by your brotherhood throughout the world.

1 Peter 5:8-9 (ESV)

D oes God really control the forces of evil in the world? This question
was hitting home for me. It was Israel 1990. We had moved there
about seven months before on assignment with the U.S. State Department. We immediately loved living in Israel. We are Jewish but we also
believe in Jesus and it was a dream come true to live in a place where the bulk
of Old and New Testament stories took place. For Jewish believers and many
other believers, there is great excitement over the fact that Israel has become
a country again which means that God is not finished with the Jews in spite
of them essentially being in exile since the year 70 A.D.

The first few months of our time there, we settled into our home in a town
north of Tel Aviv and got our children enrolled in the American International School nearby. On August 2, 1990, the president of Iraq, Saddam
Hussein, invaded Kuwait. U.S. defense forces rushed to the Persian Gulf and
the U.N. Security Council passed a resolution authorizing the use of force
against Iraq if they did not withdraw from Kuwait by January 15, 1991. In
situations like this at embassies around the world, spouses and children will
often be evacuated back to the U.S. until dangerous conflicts are resolved.
In our case, no decision had been made, but my husband was very set on
me and our three children staying for the duration. I wasn't so sure I wanted
that because I had never been through anything like this before.

Within weeks, we were issued gas masks and for our 1-year-old daughter, a gas tent. One day, I set up the gas tent and realized that when she would be placed in the tent, we could not touch her- she would be sealed in. I imagined her crying and reaching for us and us only being able to touch her through a plastic sleeve. Something about picturing that undid me. I freaked out and yelled at my husband that I wanted to be evacuated. He suggested we go out for a walk to discuss this without scaring the children.

We walked around our beautiful neighborhood with colorful bougainvillea plants flowing over every wall. My husband explained his point of view and asked me to pray about staying and trusting God with the outcome. I explained my freak-out with the gas tent and that I didn't want to stick around for bombing attacks. My husband presented his argument again, saying that he felt keeping the family together was better than for us to be separated. All of a sudden, as we were walking by a particular house, a large, vicious-looking dog charged at us, barking and baring his fangs. He came within a couple of yards of us and then his leash stopped him cold in his tracks. God spoke to me at that moment: "This is Saddam Hussein. He looks ferocious but I have him by the leash." With those words, all my fear dissolved and I told my husband I was going to trust God with the decision. It was amazing how God spoke to me so clearly through the incident with the ferocious dog so that my whole outlook on the situation had changed. My husband and I were united in our decision for me and the kids to stay.

The next day, embassy families were given a mandatory order to leave Israel, (while our working spouses were to remain behind) and in spite of the fact that Iraq threw 42 scud missiles at Israel (which my husband said were very scary), very few people were injured. I had learned an important lesson about trusting God and seeing that He has control over the forces of evil in this world. He also knows how to help us humans navigate through the scary times in our lives.

Author: Miriam Kook

REFLECTION QUESTIONS

What does it mean to you that God has Satan by a leash?

Have you ever experienced Satan being a roaring lion in your life?

How are we as believers supposed to resist him?

Intentional Choosing

So will I ever sing praise to your name, as
I perform my vows day after day.

Psalm 61:8 (ESV)

Many things crowd our to-do list. So many plans and hopes and chores and "have tos" that call to us and divide our attention. It gets noisy in our own heads and our own lives as we overplan, overstress, and overworry. Rather than competing, pressing, and straining, what if today was marked by performing our vows to Him day after day? Small increments of time gifted to us. Today. It really is all we have. No one knows what tomorrow will bring, certainly not next week or, even next year, recent years have done a good job of teaching us that one!

I open my Bible to Psalm 61. A reminder that He is the Rock higher than I. When I feel shaky or uncertain, fearful, or anxious, He comes with stability and assurance that calms and quiets my soul. He is the refuge and strong tower against the enemy. He easily sees over the head of all my enemies, the world, my own flesh, and the prince of darkness who keeps stirring up division.

The Psalmist concludes this psalm with precious words. "So will I ever sing praises to your name; as I perform my vows day after day."

Almost a Pollyanna picture of Snow White singing along as she sweeps the cottage, birds all a flutter. But the reality is, that King David wrote these words not while sweeping a cottage, but in fear, in battle. He wrote the words not as an escape from reality, but rather in the midst of it. He made the real choice to praise God in song right there in the fear-filled trials of his life, possibly during his son, Absalom's, rebellion.

How can these words ring true of us in our own life? How do we make the choice to live this out in a God-honoring way, despite the circumstance we find ourselves?

First, he makes the choice to praise God. Regardless of our pain, trial, or situation, there is always something to praise God for, because He is unchanging. He is worthy of praise. David does not sing praises for the circumstances. He sings praises for God's unchanging, everlasting name. or character.

In the hospital room, as we were saying goodbye to my Dad for the last time, the Lord brought a song to my own heart to remind me of how good and how present *He* was right in the middle of the not good pain, trial and loss.

When it is the hardest to remember His goodness, I often start running down the alphabet and praising God for attributes He brings to mind. *God, you are Amazing, Beautiful, Caring, Dad, Excellent...* We can always make the choice to see God and praise Him.

Secondly, the Psalmist makes the choice to sing. Now I am not a singer, I cannot carry a tune in a bucket, nor would anyone want me to! But when I turn up the praise music and make the choice to sing along, my mouth tells my ears what is true, and the nonsensical lies in my heart and mind begin to fade as the truth becomes louder.

Making the choice to turn on worship music in my house sets the tone for my morning and I find my heart is being led towards the Lord rather than away from it. Being intentional to sing praises, especially when we don't feel like it strengthens the faith muscle within us that ultimately leads our thoughts and actions for the day.

Ephesians 5:15-21 tells of the effects of this deliberate choice. Being filled with the Spirit rather than drunk on the world, overflows us with songs and hymns that lead us to gratitude and submission to others that would never be the case any other way.

Finally, King David makes the intentional choice to just do the next right thing, as Elisabeth Elliot has said after her missionary husband, Jim Elliot was martyred. What is the next thing? That is where David focuses as he closes this psalm. He moves forward, performing his vows to God day after day. Not jumping ahead to tomorrow's things, but rather doing them day after day. Each day being acted on as the only one before him.

Author: Mariel Davenport

REFLECTION QUESTONS

What might be your next thing?

What is before you this day to walk through and accomplish for His glory?

How might you be filled with psalms and hymns and spiritual songs that your mouth reminds your ears to focus on and then move through your day with purpose?

Wonderfully Made

For you created my inmost being; you knit me
together in my mother's womb. I praise you
because I am fearfully and wonderfully made; your
works are wonderful, I know that full well.

Psalm 139:13-14 (NIV)

've always carried a lot. A lot of care. A lot of responsibility. A lot of pain. A lot of thoughts. A lot of dreams. A lot of expectations. A lot of feelings. *Especially feelings.* Big feelings were my constant companions, the uninvited guests that would never leave, invisible bullies that pushed me around.

"You're too sensitive!"

"You're such an overreactor!"

"You need to get your emotions under control!"

Classic, chronic, overreactor became my identity, and my shame. I would look at my too-much-and-not-enough self in the mirror, exhausted from my never-ending inner war and think: *I'll never slay this dragon! I'll never be like Jesus!*

I moved through the world with a heaviness others didn't seem to have. I shouldered burdens others didn't seem to notice. On the outside, I learned the part of peace and joy and played it well, but on the inside, the battle raged. *Fight for peace* became my ironic mantra.

It wasn't until my late 30's, well into my years of mothering three high-needs children that my full armour of human-striving failed spectacularly. Sitting there in the rust of failure, my broken heart fully exposed before the Lord,

I saw for the first time how it had been wired. Fearfully. Wonderfully. Lovingly. *Intentionally.*

I began to realize that my big feelings were not my flesh working in *opposition* to the heart of God, but rather part of my unique design as a *reflection* of the heart of God, *when balanced in the light of His presence.* Rather than try to *squash* my feelings, (and becoming a pressure cooker instead), I began instead to *feel* my feelings and then *let them go.* Rather than handle my shortcomings harshly, I handled them with the same gentleness and compassion as the hands that had knit me together.

It looked something like this:

"Lord, my anger is great, but Your patience is greater."

"Lord, my disappointment is heavy, but Your grace is sufficient."

"Lord, my sorrow is deep, but Your love is deeper still."

When balanced in the light of God's presence, my shame became my strength. The part of me I was trying to put to death became beautifully resurrected and redeemed, restored to its original design. It's what allows me to enter in to the suffering and dark places of others, with compassion and hope to offer. It's what helps me to see the miracle of beauty and meaning in the every day, ordinary, unremarkable places. It's what allows me to see the beauty and artistry in *you.*

When balanced in the light of Jesus' presence,

The drive to control others becomes a passion to protect the vulnerable, revealing His power.

The fear of conflict becomes a bridge to unity, revealing His peace.

The pursuit of perfection becomes a beacon for what is good, revealing His righteousness.

The desire for what is self-serving becomes a vessel for humility, revealing His love.

The addiction to achievement becomes an inspiration for what is possible, revealing His efficacy.

The chasm of comparison becomes a wellspring of beauty and compassion, revealing His creativity.

The high place of knowledge becomes a safe place of wisdom, revealing His sovereignty.

The paralysis of fear becomes a shofar of courage, revealing His faithfulness and provision.

The gluttony for pleasure becomes a deep, stable wholeness, revealing His joy.

Our loving, patient Savior wants us to examine our unique wiring in the light of His presence, not so He can *destroy* it, but so He can *redeem* it! For He has designed you beautifully and intentionally to carry a unique aspect of His character into the world, and *He delights in you!*

Author: Jennifer Hayes

REFLECTION QUESTIONS

What part of your "wiring" have you mislabelled as "flesh" that actually hints at your unique design?

How does this lovely vulnerability become a testament to His glory?

What aspect of God's character where you made to reflect?

Spend some time in the Lord's presence with these questions. Expose your heart in His presence and ask Him to reveal and redeem your beautiful and unique design.

Fast & Pray

After Yeshua came into the house, His disciples began
questioning Him in private, 'Why couldn't we drive it out?' and
He said to them 'This kind cannot come out except by prayer.'

Mark 9:28-29 (TLV)

I felt like the walking dead. My feet seemed like lead weights on the end of my legs as I made my rounds at my job at the hospital. I had not slept more than a couple of hours each night for almost two weeks now. I was living in a new state, working a new job, and being a single mom to two little girls. Nothing was familiar and everything was hard. I figured it was the stress that was keeping me up at night, compounded by the fact that I was sleeping in the same bed with a 3-year-old and a 5-year-old. Not because we did not have another bed, but because nothing was familiar for them, and they slept peacefully with me in the middle of the two of them. Me, not so much.

At the hospital, it was my duty to inventory the nurses' stations and ER supply rooms, and make sure that they were fully stocked and rotating the supplies so that nothing expired. If it did, I was to remove and dispose of it properly. There were inventory checks and balances that I had to make sure were completed in addition to the rounds. This job required a lot of walking in the halls of the hospital and my lack of sleep was catching up to me. I caught myself seeing things that were not there in the hallways, apparitions caused by my exhaustion. One night at home, when I finally did fall asleep, I dreamed that a demon-like figure was breaking down our bathroom door while my daughters and I huddled inside of it. *Something has to change,* I thought. *I can't keep going on like this!*

As I became convinced that this was less likely to be stress and more likely a spiritual battle that I was in, I remembered the story in the Bible about the demon that the disciples of Jesus could not cast out. When they questioned Him privately about it, He told them that some demons could only be driven out by prayer. I decided right then and there to go on an intentional time of fasting and prayer until this stronghold on me was broken.

I stocked up on liquid nourishment; V-8 juice, broth, milk, and other liquids. I resolved to use the time that I would normally be eating instead in prayer and reading The Word. I sat in my car during my lunch and breaks reading my Bible and sending up prayer after prayer. It took three days of this devoted study, prayer time, and liquid fast, but on the third night, I finally slept several, dream-free hours. My fasting and prayer had done what Jesus said they would. It had driven away the tormenter and broken the enemy's hold on me, as I focused on God, His promises, and His Word. This has become a practice that I have continued throughout the years, spending time of self-sacrifice through fasting and prayer to heal my body and spirit and to hear God more clearly.

Author: Anita Stafford

REFLECTION QUESTION

Why do you think that Jesus' disciples could not drive out the demon and Jesus could?

Have you ever done a fast of any kind for spiritual reasons?

If so, what have you done? If not, have you considered it?

What was the result of your time of fasting and prayer?

Discerning His Voice

My sheep listen to my voice; I know them, and they follow me.

John 10:27 (NIV)

In all honesty, I have struggled with this facet of my faith more than any other. There have been deepest black of days, when my soul felt as if it had gone through a shredder, and I could not hear His voice, no matter how I strived in my own flesh. Prayers felt fleeting, like listless kites without a string. My tears burned hot on my cheeks, in a space as vast as a starless night. I couldn't feel His presence, sense His goodness, or know the depth of His love.

At the time, I would describe it as cruel. I would cry out in desperation, "Why God, at my darkest hour, would you abandon me?" Looking back, I know now that a mediocre sense of His love would not have rescued me from the loss of my pregnancies, the waiting for test results, the loss of a career, and so much more. Nothing less than the undeniable tether of God holding onto me for dear life, would suffice.

Because I could not sense His presence, I dug in my heels deeper, I prayed harder than I have ever prayed, worshipped more fervently, wept unceasingly, and wrestled the God of Jacob for my answer, and I would not let Him go until I felt His presence. That was the only thing that saved my life on blackest of nights, darkest of days.

It was in moments like this that I learned to recognize the voice of my Father. A gentle, calming, soothing, voice, almost too quiet to distinguish. It's the brush of hair against your cheek, a soft spring breeze, the rhythmic breathing of a baby. Any other voice, and I know I am dealing with an imposter. The voice of self-condemnation is always covered with a veil of "correction." It sounds a lot like this: "You should know better than this. I am so disappointed in you. How do you ever expect Me to use you if you keep messing up like this? How many times do you have to repeat the same lesson before you learn? Baby Christians don't even make these types of mistakes. You are such a mess. You can't even go one day without losing your patience. Fruits of the Spirit? What fruits? You are rotten through and through. Everyone can see that you are a fraud." I could continue for days; the enemy is crafty and invests all his efforts into fooling us that we are hearing the voice of God, not a wolf in sheep's clothing.

The other night, after brushing my teeth, I open the door to find my 11-year-old daughter fidgeting and in obvious distress. After several minutes of drawing her into conversation, she bursts into a ball of tears. She manages to compose herself long enough to share, "I think God is telling me to be a missionary. I don't want to be a missionary," and then returns to her uncontrollable sobs.

Truth be told, I didn't do a very good job controlling my humor. After a couple light laughs, I wrapped my arms around her and told her, "Honey, if God truly does want you to become a missionary, and I have no idea what His plans and purposes for your life are, He is not going to tell you in such a way that causes you anxiety, fear, and sadness. I know you desperately want to become a zoologist, and so, if God does intend for you to become a missionary, I would expect it to sound something like this, 'Mom, I hardly can believe it, and I know it must be from God because it's the last thing I would ever want to do, but I believe He is calling me into the mission field and I actually feel joy and excitement."

A look of relief swept over her face. I reminded her of the gentle and loving character of God; that His yoke is easy, and His burden is light, and He is a loving Father.

She was able to go to bed that night, trusting that whatever God has in store for her, she will look forward to it with joyful anticipation, not dread, fear, and an anxious spirit.

We can either hear the voice of our loving Father, reaching into the depths of our soul with words that align with His Word, the unsettling, anxious, selfish voice of our flesh, or the deceptive, condemning voice of the enemy of our souls. Whenever we are faced with a decision, we can think on these things and begin to recognize His voice above all others.

Author: Kristin Cash

REFLECTION QUESTIONS

When have you struggled to discern the voice of God above all others?

Were you able to make a decision that left you feeling peace?

Jot down some ways in which the enemy tries to convince you that he is the voice of your Father.

With All My Mind

Jesus replied, 'Love the Lord your God with all your
heart and with all your soul and with all your mind.'
This is the first and greatest commandment.

Matthew 22:37-38 (NIV)

Any personality tests that I take show that I am what is considered a "feeler" rather than a "thinker." This means I make decisions based on what I feel more than what I think. As a result, my faith was, for many years, what I think of as an emotional faith. My relationship with the Lord tended to be quite affected by my feelings. It wasn't completely based on them, but my emotions played a big part in my faith.

Then one year, God took me into a season of turmoil. I had just returned from two years on the mission field and was looking for a job. I was approached by a small Bible College about a role in their kitchen. I visited the college, had an interview and a tour, and met some of the staff over a coffee break. As I was traveling back home, I remember praying, "Lord, I don't want to be like Moses saying, 'No, don't send me there.' But I have no excitement for this job." About the same time, I had heard about a small bakery/restaurant for sale in a town where one of my brothers lived with his family. I went to visit and to check it out. I had a lot of excitement for that opportunity and things quickly came together for it. I had peace about my decision to pursue this rather than accepting the offer of employment at the Bible College. I believed this was what God wanted me to do.

As soon as I made the offer and it was accepted, the stress hit. I then entered the most difficult 10 ½ months of my life. A medical emergency in my family meant that those who wanted to support me in this venture weren't able to do that. I was alone and extremely stressed in a town where I knew almost no one. I missed the community I had enjoyed on the mission field. I would wake up in the middle of the night and be unable to go back to sleep. And I feared that I would be stuck with this small business in this small town for many years.

In the midst of all the turmoil, however, an interesting thing happened. My faith, which had always been based on my emotions, began to change. In the middle of the night, when I couldn't sleep, I knew God was there. I began to trust that the things I knew about Him and read about Him in Scripture were true regardless of what my emotions might be saying. I began to know my faith rather than just feel it. When I share about this experience, I describe it as the time when my faith went from my heart to my head. And it made my faith much stronger.

God took me out of that season in a way that was clearly Him. The business sold in seven days. The Bible College was again looking for someone in the kitchen and that year I was very excited about the possibilities of working there. When they allowed me to interview again, they asked what had changed. All I could say was, "It was God. I have no explanation for the fact that I had no excitement last year and I do this year, except that this is God's timing." When they offered me a position that year, I gladly accepted. As is so often the case, one of the most difficult seasons of my life was what I needed for me to know my faith, for my faith to become stronger and fuller. It was crucial to my faith journey.

Since that experience, I have become convinced that it is important for "feelers" to come to a place where they also know their faith. And I think it is equally important for "thinkers" to discover the emotional aspect of their faith. I believe this helps us obey the command to love Him with all our heart and with all our mind. God wants us to experience Him completely and we can't do that if we experience Him with only our heart or only our mind. As difficult and stressful as that time in my life was, it was worth it in order to receive what He gave me – the ability to know my faith, not just feel it. I want to be able to love God with all of my mind as well as all of my heart.

Author: Barb Loewen

REFLECTION QUESTIONS

Would you describe yourself as a feeler or a thinker?

What is your reaction to the idea that feelers needs to know their faith and thinkers need to feel their faith?

Are you willing to ask God to show you how to love Him with all of your heart and all of your mind? If not, what is stopping you?

Choosing Thankfulness

Be anxious for nothing, but in everything by prayer
and supplication, with thanksgiving, let your
request be known to God, and the peace of God
of which surpasses all understanding will guard
your hearts and minds through Christ Jesus.

Philippians 4:6-7 (NKJV)

Reading this verse, and what it promises almost seems too good to be true. Let's be honest, being anxious for nothing is easier said than done. There is always something to worry about unless we are living in complete denial. And being thankful for everything can be a stretch sometimes, or am I the only one honest enough to admit it? I'm not sounding very Christian, am I?

However there comes a point in all our lives when we have nothing else to lose, so why not try it?

For me one of those times arrived unexpectedly, as they often do, when my youngest son was killed in a car accident. To say that my heart was ripped out of my chest, would be an understatement. It hurt just to breathe, let alone pray and be thankful. But God!

I can say I am only alive today because of Jesus. I knew this promise by heart. I had heard, as probably many of you, it preached time and again. I had prayed and declared this promise over other areas in my life many times. But how was I to be thankful in all things including my boy dying?

Truth be told, I wasn't thankful. I was gutted. Confused, heartbroken, angry, and distraught beyond words. I remember a dear friend offering to go for a walk with me a few days after he had died. Her gesture was lovely. But I was struggling just to get out of bed and stagger to the kitchen, let alone take a walk down the road. I would never be the same. No one who has ever lost a child is.

However! If there has been one thing, I've learned in my walk with Him, it is this: there is ALWAYS something to be thankful for. Even if it's as simple as thanking Him for your next breath or for the green tree outside your window. There is always something! So that's where I started. Did I feel thankful? Not particularly. Was I still confused and wanting answers? Yes, for sure!

But I chose to believe. To believe His promise that by prayer and supplication (the act of asking for something earnestly and humbly), with thanksgiving, He would give me a peace that guards my heart and my mind. And He did just that.

I didn't get the answers to my questions. I stopped asking why and chose to trust Him. His divine peace continues to guard my heart and mind to this day. I am truly thankful for so many things that happened and are continuing to happen throughout our grief journey. Like the love of family and friends from all around the world that continues to surround us to this day. Or the legacy that our son has left behind, a life that has impacted so many more people than we ever realized. And the goodness and love of a Father in Heaven, accompanied by His supernatural peace that has consistently enveloped us and never left us.

So yes, it is easier said than done. And being thankful for everything does stretch us. But oh, the peace it brings! Surpassing anything we could have ever hoped for, dreamed of, or thought of in our wildest imaginations!

Be encouraged today my friend, His promises are true! His peace is our guard, our fortress, and our strength. Choose to be thankful when it's easier said than done.

It is definitely worth it.

Author: Kim Beaumont

REFLECTION QUESTIONS

What are three things that you can be thankful for today?

How has His peace in the past helped guard your heart and mind?

The Shackles of My Eating Disorder

For he has rescued us from the kingdom of darkness and transferred us into the Kingdom of his dear Son...

Colossians 1:13 (NLT)

It didn't happen all at once. It came in like a thief in the night when I was least aware of the danger. I cannot, despite much soul-searching and praying, decipher an exact moment when the eating disorder took hold, and now that I am rescued from the kingdom of darkness, I'm not sure it makes much of a difference. Jesus redeemed me.

While pregnant with my oldest daughter, now 14, I became incredibly sensitive to my ever-changing body. Morning sickness blended into evening sickness, which kept me stumbling for the bathroom all hours of the night. My appetite wasn't kind to me.

Eventually, the nausea left as abruptly as it came, and I was able to return to my normal activities. Summer months rolled in, and the closer I came to her due date, the more the pounds compounded. One day, in late May, while visiting family in New York, I became distinctly aware of the alarming size of my joints. Within days, I was diagnosed with preeclampsia.

The day I gave birth to my 37-week, 5 pound bundle of love, I weighed 90 pounds heavier than my prepregnancy weight.

Postpartum depression kicked in, and although the weight was slowly coming off, I felt determined to return to my healthier state, so I signed up for a Fitness Competition and went to work.

The day I competed, I was attending an awards ceremony, when a fellow competitor, 10 years into their fitness career, found humor in my naive understanding of the addiction I had stumbled upon. I found it disturbing that she was completely deferential to her visibly underweight frame.

The next five years were a state of half survival as I found myself submitting to the vice of the scale. My body fought for every pound, while I found ways to ignore the gnawing in my stomach and my soul, purging every bit of nutrition, physically and spiritually.

I built a cavern of darkness around my mind, so my conscience was stifled; my life, so my actions were not questioned; my eyes, so the mirror became what I wanted it to become.

Until one night, after the scale tipped under 100 pounds, I was lying in bed, shivering under heaps of blankets, while my heart pounded in my chest. It was in that moment that I heard the voice of Jesus, speaking tenderly to my soul, that I was on the verge of losing my life if I didn't choose to reach out for help.

The next morning, I saw the first crack of light, as Jesus held my hand and walked me through the doors of an outpatient counseling center for eating disorders. I began a very long, arduous battle for my life as the pounds returned, the scale was thrown away, and my soul was freed from the shackles of darkness.

Physically I was freed, and spiritually I was redeemed.

Author: Kristin Cash

REFLECTION QUESTIONS

How can you relate to this story?

Have you ever found yourself in a self-made prison?

Can you acknowledge a time when Jesus rescued you from yourself?

The Good, the Rebellious, & the Redeemed

O give thanks to the Lord, for he is good, for his
steadfast love endures forever! Let the redeemed of
the Lord say so, whom he has redeemed from trouble,
and gathered in from the lands, from the east, and
from the west, from the north and from the south.

Psalm 107:1-3 (NKJV)

I grew up a rancher's daughter on the high plains and mountain ranges of Wyoming. The rugged landscape and big western sky of God's creation has always inspired and thrilled me. The ranch I grew up on was the perfect setting for three kids enjoying adventure and mischief; a place for my brothers and I to let our imaginations run wild. It was also a refuge and retreat as I was growing up, where I found God in the quiet tranquility of the land. It's where He brought comfort and peace to my sometimes ragged soul.

I didn't have to look any further than our back door to know that God was a Master Creator. I saw His presence in every aspect of creation and was captivated by it. Wyoming sunrises displayed with their brilliant oranges, reds, pinks and purples over the mountains, the miracle of new life every calving season, and an unending variety of plants and animals. It delighted my senses and brought joy to my soul. He could have simply created the world to sustain us and no more, making the entire earth a dull combination of browns and greys with no color, sound or smell. But instead, the Master Creator chose to create beauty and variety.

My mother explained to me that God created us to thrive in fellowship with Him because He loves and desires an intimate, personal relationship with us. But I struggled with why He would want a relationship with me. I was messy and mean, I didn't always make the right choices or obey my parents, I lied, picked on my brothers, and was selfish. I worked hard at being good so He wouldn't suddenly decide I wasn't worth loving. I relied on my own "goodness" and strengths not His, and eventually I'd mess up. With each failure, I faced discouragement because I wasn't good enough on my own.

By the time I started college, I was weary from trying so hard but failing. I felt like a huge disappointment to everyone who loved me, especially God. I decided that, since I obviously couldn't be good enough, I'd settle with being bad enough, and I began to rebel against God and my parents. But this was just as exhausting as trying to be good. It was an empty and shallow way to live, and I grew more depressed and discouraged by my lack of self-control and self-destructive behavior. Because of poor choices I soon found myself home on academic probation; I felt that redemption was beyond my reach.

This was where the good girl and the rebel collided. I was lost and confused, filled with regret and shame. I realized I needed to figure out what it was that I truly believed, and what I wanted my life to reflect. One day I walked out to a large rock that sat in the middle of one of our pastures. I climbed up onto it and cried out to the Lord, pouring my heart and my hurts out to Him. Sitting there on that huge rock, I felt His presence cover me and was reminded of the words in Psalm 18:2 (NKJV), "The Lord is my rock and my fortress and my deliverer; My God, my strength, in whom I will trust; my shield and the horn of my salvation, my stronghold." God wasn't some distant, uncaring God; He was a personal Savior, the Lord Jesus, who hurt when I hurt, held all my tears, knew my failures and longed for me to draw near to Him. He wanted me to put my hope and trust in Him and not in my own abilities.

I recognized that, just as I could never be good enough to save myself from perishing in my sins, neither could I be so bad that I was beyond saving. No matter what I had done or how far I had rebelled against Him, God desperately wanted me to see my worth in Him. I was not a hopeless cause. He loved me enough to save me, despite my sin, right there in the midst of it, not waiting until I was good enough and deserved saving. He redeemed that good little girl, and that rebellious young lady and brought me into a right relationship with Him through His Son. As a result of being His redeemed, I will spend the rest of my life telling of His steadfast love.

Author: Jana Fraley

REFLECTION QUESTIONS

Do you relate with either feeling you are the one responsible for redeeming yourself, or that you are too bad to ever find redemption from God?

What is it that you believe and know to be true about the character of God?

Have you shared your own story of redemption with others?

Rebuilding Ancient Ruins

They shall build the ancient ruins; they shall raise up
the former devastations; they shall repair the ruined
cities, the devastations of many generations.

Isaiah 61:4 (ESV)

My knuckles were turning white as I gripped the steering wheel, unsure if it was anger or fear that was making my heart race. Another argument, more yelling, hurt feelings, and feelings of: *Why did we ever decide to get married?* We are far too different, far too much baggage, far too needy. And now here we are, seventeen months into this marriage contract. Even more, we are four months into parenting this new baby boy.

How could I think a baby might help heal this new marriage?

The sleepless nights and wearisome days have only intensified the emotions that feel like tidal waves. How bad could it be to end a marriage that is less than two years old? I mean we had both seen divorce in our families of origin, weren't we bound for the same anyway?

Shaking the thoughts from my head, I came to a stop sign and paused to gaze at the sky. Maybe there is a different way. In those moments, the words of my coworker came back to me about a Savior she knew, One who redeemed, transformed, and met her in her hallow, hard places.

The sleeping newborn made a noise in his carseat and I wondered at the weight of the choices before me. This little one, so helpless and dependent. Me, a mama, but only barely an adult myself, how could I make the best choices for him?

I looked up again, God, *if you are who You say You are, will You forgive me? Change me and redeem the mess before me?*

Nothing really seemed to happen visually. But somehow, I knew.

> "The LORD will guide you continually and satisfy your desire in scorched places and make your bones strong; you shall be like a watered garden, like a spring of water, whose waters do not fail. And your ancient ruins shall be rebuilt; you shall rise up the foundations of many generations; you shall be called the repairer of the breach, the restorer of streets to dwell in" (Isaiah 58:11-12, ESV).

Forgive my pride, Lord, forgive my self-righteousness.

I turned towards home with a fresh resolve. Somehow, I knew God was already there when my man met me in the yard with grace.

The twenty years since that day have not been easy, but God has been present, the marriage is redeemed, and that little boy grew to be a mighty man of God, purely by the grace and goodness of a God who builds up ancient ruins and former devastations in new generations.

Author: Mariel Davenport

REFLECTION QUESTIONS

What generational sins are you currently carrying?

How can you lift those to the Lord and repent of your part in that? Then move forward in the grace and forgiveness of God.

What Does God Expect of Me?

As a father has compassion on his children,
So the Lord has compassion on those who fear him;
For he knows how we are formed,
He remembers that we are dust.

Psalm 103:13-14 (NIV)

still remember the day I won the fight, but lost the war. I was in a screaming match with my son. Again. He could not follow the simplest instructions. Everything was a fight. Everything was hard. Everything was on fire.

I was consumed by my anger, frustration, exhaustion, disappointment, and hopelessness. I was overwhelmed, I was drowning, and I was screaming.

My son ran to his room and slammed the door. I could hear him in there pounding his pillow while he raged. I stood in the kitchen, head in my arms on the counter. *"I can't do this, Lord! I can't parent this child! You picked the wrong girl and I'm failing!"*

That's when he showed me the picture. In my mind I saw my son, sitting in a wheelchair at the bottom of the stairs, and me, yelling at him to climb them. *It's not that hard! Just climb the stairs! Why won't you just climb the stairs!* His head and shoulders slumped low.

With my head in arms on the countertop, sobbing, I begged, pleaded with Jesus to help me. I just could not get control of my emotions. I could not control my anger. No matter how hard I tried, I just couldn't seem to grasp the peace he had promised. No matter how hard I tried, I just could not become like him. There must be something wrong with me, some deep, irredeemable flaw preventing the transformation I longed for.

I understood the purpose of the thorn in Paul's side, but *this?* This thorn of mine was harming my children! *Why wouldn't he take it?*

Lord! Why won't you take this thorn away? What a profound disappointment I must be.

Then another picture came. It was me as a little girl, trying to reach something on the top shelf of the cupboard. No matter how hard I tried, how high I jumped, I couldn't reach it.

The Lord said: "Am I disappointed in her because she can't reach it?" No. She's too little, that's not a fair expectation. "And neither am I disappointed in you when you cannot reach what is too high. I already know the outcome. I remember that you are dust, and I am the only One who can hold the dust together. I am the only One who can provide what is too high."

In that moment, I realized not only my unfair expectations of my son, but the unfair expectations I held for myself, but believed where God's expectations of me. But what do we expect of dust? *Not much.*

The God who formed me from the dust is the only One who can hold me together, the only One who can breathe life into the dry and dirty spaces, and the only One who can make it clean.

That day in the kitchen, when I surrendered my fruitless striving, my hopeless reaching, into the hands of the One who holds all things, the dry dust became moist clay, and real work began.

Author: Jennifer Hayes

REFLECTION QUESTIONS

What do you think God expects of you?

What "high things" are you trying to reach?

Do you believe that God has compassion for you? Why or why not?

Close your eyes and ask your Father for your own picture. What does he show you?

Where Demons Tread

For our struggle is not against flesh and blood, but
against the rulers, against the powers, against the
worldly forces of this darkness, and against the spiritual
forces of wickedness in the heavenly places.

Ephesians 6:12 (TLV)

I held my son in my arms and stood at the window looking at the cloud on the horizon. Something did not look quite right about that storm gathering in the distance. There was a glow to it, something unusual in the way that the light played out, ebbing, and flowing almost like a living entity. My spirit within me was troubled and anxious. I stood riveted to that spot, wanting to leave the window, but afraid to take my eyes off the coming disturbance.

As the disruption in the weather came closer, I began to hear the noise. A clashing sound, like metal on metal, accompanied it. This was not like any storm that I had ever seen before. I tightened the hold on my infant son in my arms as fear began to take root deep within me.

As the cloud of dust and noise came closer, I realized this was not a weather disturbance at all, but an accumulation of bodies, running ever and ever closer to this little house that we huddled in, just my son and I, alone and unprotected.

When they came close enough that I could make out figures, I found myself frozen in terror. These were not earthly beings, not a herd of animals or people, but something else, something more evil and sinister than my eyes had ever gazed upon. This was a demonic horde, and their target was us.

I spun away from the window and looked around me for protection, a weapon, anything with which to defend my son and myself. There was nothing in the room but a sofa. I flew across the room, behind the sofa and flipped it over. We hid behind it using it as a shield. The house started to shake and the dust began to filter in through the open window. They would be here soon. But they would not take us easily. I would defend my son to the death, and they would not find us as weak a prey as they thought we would be. My last conscious thought was of the sheer evil that I saw in their features as the demons from hell began to pour in through the open window.

I woke in a cold sweat, gasping for breath at the vividness of the dream and the pounding of my heart. I was safe, and more importantly, my son was safe. It took a long, long time for my troubled spirit to calm down, a time of whispered prayers and thanksgiving that it was only a dream.

Later that same day, I gathered with other women from our small church in a Bible study that I had only recently started attending. When they went around the room asking for prayer requests, I shared with them my dream and asked this group of believers what they thought about it. One of the older women was thoughtful for a moment before she replied. "You are in a fight for your son's soul. The demons represent the forces that will come to bear against you and your son for his eternal soul. The impending battle in your dream represents the battle that you will face as you raise him. Be aware that there are forces trying to take your child and all our children away from us. This is our mission as mothers... to teach them the things of the Lord and to protect them."

I have always remembered that dream so vividly as time has shown me that we truly are in a spiritual battle for our children's souls. Do not take lightly your prayers and the power that you have as a mother to fight the forces of evil that we battle with for the lives and souls of our children.

Author: Anita Stafford

REFLECTION QUESTIONS

Have you ever felt like you were in spiritual battle?

If you are a mother, have your children accepted Jesus as their Lord and Savior?

How can you be praying for your children, whether they are still young or adults?

Breath of Heaven

My mouth shall speak the praise of Yahweh:
and let all flesh bless His holy name.

Psalm 145:21 (WEB)

My son Jameson was a modern-day miracle. Everything about his conception, survival in the womb, and first gasping breath. Nothing short of the hand of God, moving on his behalf. His middle name, Jack, translated is 'God is gracious." And that He is.

If you have already read my testimony of redemption from the grip of an eating disorder, you can recall that I had a six-and-a-half-year absence of my monthly cycle. Literally the opposite of the woman in the Bible who bled consistently for years upon years. I lacked even the slightest evidence of femininity for six and a half years. Until one month, just before Christmas, I was feeling off, and threw my heart's caution to the wind, by taking a pregnancy test, which to my shock, was unquestionably positive. Not only did I not have a cycle for months prior to his conception, but, every baby I carry requires I take high doses of progesterone from three weeks onward, and this little guy was already baking away for 8.5 weeks.

Our first ultrasound revealed a sweet, miniature little guy, with no viable heartbeat. Absolutely terrifying, given my past, and subsequent future. By God's grace, the next week, after dragging my fear laden feet into my appointment, we were again shocked to hear the whoosh whoosh of his steady little heart, beating away, reminding me that God still answers impossible prayers.

Carrying him was pure bliss. My two older girls were self-sufficient, so I was able to put my feet up, and soak in every magical moment. We were all swimming in bliss, until the terrifying moment that my undiagnosed hematoma burst and bled for nearly a week, threatening me with a blood transfusion and limited mobility. Still, we again held out weary hands to the God who places gracious miracles into our lives, and breathes courage into our very souls.

Lightheartedly, and with a world of expectations, I planned for my VBAC, thanking God that my little guy was being cooperative, and resting head down, until the day before my attempted labor trial, when he flipped our world upside down, by flipping his birthday ready body head up. Way, way up, in fact. So high, that the next day would reveal a very life-threatening delivery. To us both.

Lying back on the stiff surgical bed, I again found myself holding my breath. A maternal nurse, in heart and duty, reminded me how important it was for me to take slow, steady breaths. Air in, air out, of the same lungs God delicately wove together in my dependent body.

Surgery began, and I found myself surprisingly wrapped up in all the details; the smell of the room and the latex, the stark brightness of each overhead light, the murmur of each attendant, and the obstetricians performing the surgery. The air was full of a joyful anticipation, as the surgeons chattered away about my previous deliveries and condition of my incision sites. In one abrupt moment, I heard my OB say, "Baby's head is lodged. There's no fluid remaining in the sac, and I cannot release him. I need to do a full transverse quickly." The environment entirely changed, and everyone became silent, as my surgeon worked quickly to release the baby. With a sudden jerk and splash of fluid, he said, "He's out. I've got him. He needs to breath." The pediatrician swooped him up, and rushed to a table where my husband met her, lightly touching our son's small, motionless hand, praying childlike prayers for the breath of Heaven to enter our little boy's lungs.

Silence. Waiting. Silence.

You could hear a pin drop in that space as we all held space for God to answer. Waiting on bated breath for this one breath that would shatter the suffocating stillness. In an instant, as sudden as the fear surrounding the moment, my son drew in a long, boisterous gasp, followed by the unmistakable sound of a newborn's cry.

Yahweh is translated to YHWH. It is the aspirated consonants that, when spoken, create the sound of our breathing. To breathe is to speak the name of God. To breath in YH, and to exhale WH. It's in the very breaths we take, each moment, of each day, since the heralding cry of a baby, that utter the name of our God. When my son finally took those long-awaited breaths, he was indeed praising God for his very existence. Heaven on Earth; Breath of Heaven.

Author: Kristin Cash

REFLECTION QUESTIONS

Take time to study the power of YHWH. Listen to the sound of your breathing and how it utters His name.

When was a moment you needed to remind yourself to breathe? Did breathing instantly invite His peace?

Recognizing Your Season

For everything there is a season,
A time for every activity under heaven.
A time to be born and a time to die.
A time to plant at a time to harvest.
A time to kill and a time to heal.
A time to tear down at a time to build up.
A time to cry at a time to laugh.
A time to grieve and a time to dance.
A time to scatter stones at a time together stones.
A time to embrace and a time to turn away.
A time to search at a time to quit searching.
A time to keep at a time to throw away.
A time to tear and a time to mend.
A time to be quiet and a time to speak.
A time to love at a time to hate.
A time for war and a time for peace.

Ecclesiastes 3:1-8 (NLT)

Being an empty nester, I'm still adjusting to a quiet home. However, I'm not sure if it's the quiet house that disturbs me as much as the emptiness I sometimes feel in my heart. And even as I reflect on that, I struggle to fathom the reason for this feeling inside of me. Part of it I'm sure is the unending grief of losing a child, that I know will be there forever more. But it's not just that. Twenty-two months into the journey and I know now. However unbelievable I thought it at the time, my capacity to carry pain and heartache has increased. I know that may sound depressing, but it's not unlike love.

When I was pregnant with my second child, I worried immensely that I would not be able to love him as much as I loved his older sister. And then

I set eyes on him. The moment I heard his cry, my heart exploded with love for him. The lie that I believed instantly vaporized. I realized with instant clarity that love does not have a limit or capacity. It does not stop at one or two or three. It is unending, limitless, and knows no bounds.

Pain and grief are often on the flipside of love. That became ever so apparent when we lost Cody. I realized the depth of grief we experience parallels the love for what we have lost. Grief, like love has a continuity that accompanies life. However, it's what we *do* with that pain that results in the life we want to live. It may come on us unexpectedly, or it can be a gradual process, but either way, HOW we deal with it will manifest in our daily lives, whether we want it to or not.

To be honest, I'm not naturally a super introspective touchy-feely kind of person. As a Type A my 'go to' is *suck it up and move on*. Although this has helped achieve goals and get things done, it has not always worked well for my emotional or mental health.

One advantage of living life is that hopefully we can learn from our mistakes. Thankfully, God has a grace for that. And being a person who wants to make their life count, I'm determined to learn something from the different seasons I live through.

Recognizing the season we are in is a major key to living life well. Maybe you are surrounded by littles at the moment, or you are busy building your career. Or perhaps you have hormonal teenagers in your home, and you spend most of your life in the car. Or maybe like me, the house is somewhat quieter and you're figuring out what life looks like now. However, no matter what season we are in, there will still be pain and grief to process amongst all the joys and busyness of life.

I am learning to acknowledge when there is pain in my heart, rather than distract myself, get busy, or just flat out medicate it. For me, that can look like going to a movie, designing something, reading a book, or if I'm really desperate-going shopping.

Living a purposeful life, means leaving intentionally. So, I would like to share some of my tips on processing pain.

Pause. Take a breath, make space, and give yourself permission to check in with your heart.

Acknowledge. Ask God, is there anything in my heart that needs to be dealt with?

Ask. Ask good questions. What is the pain? Where did it come from? How is it manifesting in my life?

Embrace. Identify any lies you are believing. Remember if there is an area in your life where you have no hope, then you are believing a lie. Ask God what is His truth about that situation.

Action. Take one step today towards living out that truth.

That's the beauty of knowing Jesus. We don't have to do this living life thing alone. And as cliché as it sounds there is always a light at the end of the tunnel, even if it is but a flicker. As we turn our eyes and heart towards the light, and we take one step at a time, it shines a path for us.

God is not limited. He lives outside of time. Pain and mess do not scare Him. He promises to work all things out for our good. He is patient and kind and never leaves us, even in the dark. Because where there is light no darkness can stand. And I would rather stand and take one step towards the light, than grapple around alone in the dark. How about you?

Author: Kim Beaumont

REFLECTION QUESTIONS

Do you need to just pause and breathe?

What is one truth you can hold onto today?

What is one step you can take towards leaving out that truth?

Sometimes the Answer is No

PART ONE

Death wrapped its ropes around me; the terrors of the
grave overtook me. I saw only trouble and sorrow.

Psalm 116:3 (NLT)

Growing up, I held two dreams, the hopeful ambition that motivated all my decisions to become an astronaut, and the inner soulful song which drew me towards motherhood and rearing a large brood of children. Five to be exact. I prayed for five children, and even now, as I raise my five living children, the passion and pursuit of future pregnancies and more children is just as strong as it ever was. It's hard to express the size of our family without giving honor to the daughter and son who couldn't share our table; the two waiting in Heaven. You will see me refer to my living children as our earthly children.

In 2018, just before the 1st birthday of our fourth earthly child, I was completely overcome by the desire to conceive another baby. It was all consuming. The powerful urge within my soul was a companion to every thought I had throughout the day. I could not go one moment without acknowledging this strong desire. So much so that I told my husband I wanted to try again for another baby. To my delight, he obliged, and all the fertility supplies were ordered. My planning for pregnancies is a very methodical and well-laid process. To our shock, we conceived our first month of trying, and my heart instantly fell in love with the little life represented by the beautiful double line on that pregnancy test.

Just as quickly as the conception, so also came a torrent of fear and angst that could not be explained. I feared this sweet baby had a death sentence lingering over them. It was unrelenting and depressing. I could not swing into the blissfulness of my budding belly, because every passing thought was accompanied by distress and concern. Every morning began with another pregnancy test, as I compared the double line to the day before, gathering opinions from every member of my family, desperate to ensure baby was thriving and hormones were increasing as they should. The lines told the story of a bright and promising future with the precious one joining our family, but my heart could not settle, and my mind would not relax.

Each of my pregnancies has held some form of trauma, and for this reason, blood tests throughout are a necessity. The commute back and forth to the lab for more results became a normal part of our schedules, but each result brought on another torrent of concern, and within a few weeks, my fears were realized. My hormone levels, although increasing, were showing signs of anomaly, and my research lead me to believe he had a genetic defect referred to as Trisomy 22. Our first ultrasound showed a sweet little one, effortlessly floating around in the safety of his amniotic fluid, without a heartbeat. I was absolutely devastated, but I was sure he was there, both physically and spiritually, so I pressed in for my miracle, and was gifted with just that. Our next ultrasound told a further story as he had grown, but not proportionately, and although his heart was beating, which was priceless music to my ears, it was not as strong and steady as they hoped to see. He also had a misshapen amniotic sac and a very enlarged yolk sac which re-fused to absorb. His body was rejecting the nutrients it offered, which would enable him to rely solely on a placenta for nourishment. I knew in my heart that my research was correct, and this sweet little one would be joining his sister in Heaven. I was absolutely crushed and beyond reasoning. I wanted to believe that my Lord would rush to the rescue, heal the disease, and re-store the peace to our home which had disappeared the moment that double line appeared.

But He did not answer in the way I had hoped. Sometimes the answer is no. The technician explained to us that our son was "not compatible with life" and would not survive outside the womb. He may continue to thrive in the womb for days, weeks, or months even, but once born, would not have the organ support to live. I continued to carry our sweet miracle, until

Christmas Eve 2018 when the bleeding began. Ultrasound revealed his heart had stopped beating several days prior, and my heart ceased to beat with a zest for life that same moment. After collecting his little body for testing to confirm our suspicions, I fell into a chasm of depression. I was numb and unable to provide motherly nurturing to the rest of our earthly children. It was a debilitatingly lonely season for all of us. My marriage began to suffer the effects of withdrawal, and to this day, we are still healing from the distance that grew between us.

Author: Kristin Cash

REFLECTION QUESTIONS

Have you experienced distancing in close relationships when walking through a season of grief?

Has the Lord gently held you up during moments of uncertainty and sadness?

Have you allowed the Lord to usher you into seasons of healing?

Sometimes the Answer is No

PART TWO

Then I called on the name of the Lord: "Please, LORD, save me!" How kind the LORD is! How good He is! So merciful, this God of ours! The LORD protects those of childlike faith; I was facing death, and He saved me. Let my soul be at rest again, for the LORD has been good to me. He has saved me from death, my eyes from tears, my feet from stumbling. And so I walk in the LORD'S presence as I live here on Earth.

Psalm 116:4-9 (NLT)

Four months after his loss, we were packing for a family vacation, which I was resisting with my core. I was bitter and resentful, and didn't want to stumble upon the joys I once knew, but my sweet children were suffering, and I felt the Lord calling me into a place of healing and acceptance. Gently He drew me in, and I stopped resisting Him.

The beginning of my release began with this letter I wrote to our son, Abraham. *"Dear Abraham, Mama misses you even though I didn't get to hold your tiny fingers. I'm gonna try to live without the grief and let Jesus be the Helper of my soul. Brighter days must come for me, because that's what you would want for me, and you're living among The Light of the World. If you could, send down some extra cheer for me. Help me let go of the guilt of moving on, the heartache is too deep to carry any longer. I love you and I'm so thankful you didn't have to carry the earthly burden of your condition. Where you are, there is no pain, no trisomy, no disorder. You are whole and full of life. I'll always be your Mama. One day, I'll see you face to face. Until then, help me live a little brighter and be a good Mama to your siblings here. Give your sister up there a huge hug from me and run to your heart's content. Love always, Mama."*

I spent some time alone with the Lord in prayer and asked Him to do what only He could, and allow me to walk forward, my grief as a companion, instead of staying stagnant, a companion with death. And He did just that. He gave the courage to take one step after another, and I began smiling again, bringing hope and joy to my sweet kiddos. It was healing to see them smiling with relief, with hope in the spirits that mama had returned to her normal self, and wouldn't spend all day in tears.

Vacation was truly a gift of healing from the Lord, and provided space and time for light to creep back into my once dark soul. I allowed Him to minister to my hurt places, laden with confusion and fear. I allowed myself the luxury of smiles and laughter, and spent our vacation taking candid photographs of our kids splashing in the ocean, playing in the pool, eating picnic lunches, and having fun. The last Sunday of our trip was Mother's Day and I woke feeling grateful, joyful, and slightly nauseous. Before getting on with the morning, I humored myself by taking the last pregnancy test I owned, and to my shock, it was positive. I could hardly believe my eyes. Could God really have planted life right in the middle of loss and grief? I stumbled upon it like a flower pushing its way out of snow.

I could have walked out the next several months in fear and uncertainty, but God was nearer than my heart beating in my chest. The schedule was still full to bursting with doctor's appointments and blood panels, but it was not overcome by anxious thoughts. Although we were all on the edge of our seats, waiting the long nine months until her arrival, we were still able to enjoy the process, and walk in hope for a future. He truly does give us a future and a hope.

At 33 weeks, we found that baby would need to be born early, and while I didn't want to exactly process the idea of another premature baby, I knew that my heart could fully be at ease once I held my miracle in my arms; the culmination of a year and a half of heartache. I wanted to hear her cry, smell her head, and rub my lips on her forehead. I found ways to enjoy the final weeks of my pregnancy by meal prepping, prepping our home, and prepping my heart for the gracious and unexpected gift God had given us.

The morning Harmony Anne was born, she was 35.5 weeks. I was surrounded by a large team of people ready to assist in my pressing medical needs, and a pediatric team ready to offer support. Bright lights, cold hands, and the constant reminder that I was not in control. While there were countless reasons to fear, I had been taught, by God's ever constant presence over the last several months, that He was in control and could be trusted. After a very long, yet uneventful surgery, they drew her little body out, prepared to offer oxygen and a refuge in the NICU. But God had heard my cries for His intervention. She was born strong, hearty, and healthy, needing no intervention or assistance. In a few short moments, she was placed in my arms and I have been praising God ever since. He redeems us from the snares of death, darkness, and discouragement. He places lilies in our valleys. He is faithful, to the very end.

Author: Kristin Cash

REFLECTION QUESTIONS

Recall the times when God has redeemed you from sadness.

Have you shared your story with others to offer hope and encouragement?

If you are in a season of darkness, offer up these tears to God and thank Him in advance for the redemption He will bring.

Pick-Up Vines

I am the true vine, and my Father is the gardener. He cuts off every branch in me that bears no fruit, while every branch that does bear fruit he prunes so that it will be even more fruitful.

John 15:2 (NIV)

We had been married a little over a year when my husband and I took a short trip to Niagara on the Lake with my parents. Besides the amazing Niagara Falls themselves, this beautiful little corner of southern Ontario is also home to a flourishing wine industry, a rich environment for raising vineyards.

We had the opportunity to visit one of these vineyards, a smaller one, owned and run by 3 couples. Since we happened to be the only ones on the tour that day, our guide spent extra time with us, answering all our questions, indulging our jokes and enjoying our genuine interest in the process of tending a vineyard and producing wine.

It was not only fascinating, but enlightening! I had read John 15 countless times in my life, always a little confused about the "cutting off" part in verse 2. What did it mean? If I didn't produce fruit, would God cut me off and throw me away? It seemed to conflict with other passages like "nothing can separate us from Christ," and "none shall be plucked from my hand." I stuffed my discomfort down deep where it wouldn't cause any trouble, but still, uncertainty lurked quietly by.

I listened to our tour guide explain how vines are tended, how sometimes the vine's branches get tangled up underneath the plant. Branches that can't get sunlight can't produce fruit at best and are vulnerable to disease at worst. The branch's potential to fruit bear is far too valuable to waste the branch, so instead, to get the best fruit out of the whole plant, those branches are untangled, lifted up, cleaned off and fixed to a trellis, exposing them to the sunlight. A branch cannot bear fruit in the shade, *it must be in the sun.*

As it turns out, the original Greek word translated as "cut off" in verse 2 is *"airo,"* which actually means *"to lift up; to raise; to expose."*[3]

As I listened and watched our companion tenderly and affectionately handle his prized vines with such pride and care, understanding dawned.

When I abide in Him, He will not leave me in the shade to wither. He will lift me up out of the mud, and expose me to the light. Not so I will be embarrassed or ashamed, but so I can produce much fruit.

This is the life of sanctification. Bringing hidden things to light so we can flourish. Pruning back the flourishing things so we can explode with abundance. It's uncomfortable, this process, painful even. But our loving vinedresser is tender and patient, affectionate and attentive, and the work He begins, He completes, for the vine cannot train up itself. *Nor can the vine produce fruit without the Son.*

Author: Jennifer Hayes

REFLECTION QUESTIONS

Are there any areas in your life where you know you are not producing fruit?

Are there areas where you feel like you're being pruned?

Take a few minutes in prayer to expose these things to the Lord. Ask Him to help you submit to His work of producing abundant fruit in you.

Use What Your Daddy Gave You

For You have created my conscious, You knit me together
in my mother's womb. I praise You, for I am awesomely,
wonderfully made! Wonderful are your works—and my soul
knows that very well. My frame was not hidden from You
when I was made in the secret place, when I was woven
together in the depths of the earth, Your eyes saw me when
I was unformed and in Your book were written the days that
were formed—when not one of them had come to be.

Psalm 139: 14-16 (TLV)

It was quite the pity party that I was having, sitting in my bathroom in the dark at 2:30 in the morning. My traitorous thoughts were circling in my consciousness like a flock of vultures waiting to descend and devour me. I did not know what had woken me, only that my mind had kicked in and those circling thoughts refused to allow me to go back to sleep. We know these thoughts well; the reminders of what did not get done yesterday; the multitude of things that need to get done when the sun comes up or before; the hurtful words that someone spoke, either intentionally or not; the painful reminders of all the things that we are not or do not do good enough but should. I do not think any of us are immune to these not so friendly companions that tend to keep us company in the wee hours of the morning. For me, this day, after listening to these thoughts for far too long, I began to moan and complain to God about all the areas where I was lacking in my life. They say that comparison is the thief of joy and let me tell you, at this moment, comparison was in full riot gear and joy was on an all-out retreat. God let me go on like this for awhile, telling Him all about how I was lacking and why couldn't He make me more like everyone else? To make it more painful, one of my complaints in this tirade I was having, involved a ministry that I had a visible role in and my feelings of inadequacy compared to others that I serve alongside.

When I finally quit throwing those complaints to God like darts at a dartboard and my mind quieted enough to hear His voice, He gently asked, "What DO you like about yourself?" That question stumped me for a moment and I had to give it some thought. "Well," I replied. "I like my hair. I have pretty green eyes. I am strong physically. I am really organized." I will never forget what God said next. He replied, "Then use what your Daddy gave you." I was stunned, speechless, totally speechless. Then right there in my bathroom, out loud, I said "God, did you just say, 'use what your Daddy gave you'?" "Yes," he said. "Use what your Daddy gave you." With that one statement, those circling, traitorous vultures were silenced, at least for that day. God had given me a profound vision of how to live my life.

So often in my management career, the upper echelons of business, wanted me to focus on the weakness of my team members. I was supposed to "fix" their weakness and my own, to make us more competent, more valuable employees. But God had a different directive. Take my strengths, your strengths and work them, I mean really work them to their fullest potential. In Song of Songs 4:7 NIV, the bridegroom (God) says "you are altogether beautiful, my darling; there is no flaw in you." If God created us and He says that there is no flaw in us, then are we allowing Him to have the final word, or are we allowing the vultures of doubt and comparison tell us who and what we are? Now, I know what you are saying! Yes, there are things that all of us can work on. As a health coach and personal trainer, I make a living helping people replace bad health habits with good ones and learn to be the strongest they can be, mentally, physically, and spiritually. This is about taking good care of the temple that is your body and the home of The Holy Spirit. My desire is that everyone lives a thriving life and fulfills the God-given assignments that we all have. After all, our lives, and the way that we live them should point people to Christ and bring God glory. What I believe God wants us to do is search our hearts, listen to His voice, and understand what are the strengths and talents that He gifted us with, those things that make us unique from everyone else and work those to their fullest potential. After all, He made us, He formed our innermost parts. He certainly knows the gifts and talents that He gave us and what they are to be used for. So instead of bemoaning what we are not and what we do not have, how much would our life radically change if we focused not only on the spiritual gifts and strengths that God gave us, but on who we are in Christ, and how to use those gifts and that knowledge to bring Glory to Him?

Author: Anita Stafford

REFLECTION QUESTIONS

Have you ever had a "pity party" with yourself in the middle of the night?

What strengths and talents has God gifted you with that you may not have developed yet?

How can you use these to bring glory to God?

Notes

1. "You Are My God" by John Foley, SJ, OCP Publications, 5536 NE Hassalo Portland, OR 97213, 1970, 1996

2. Lewis, C S, and Pauline Baynes. The Lion, the Witch, and the Wardrobe. New York, NY: HarperTrophy, 1994. Print.

3. "Airo." *Bible Study Tools.* https://www.biblestudytools.com/lexicons/greek/nas/airo.html. Accessed 2021 Feb 23.

Made in the USA
Columbia, SC
13 October 2021

46651596R00231